THE GOSPEL

of

LUKE

By A. B. SIMPSON

Founder of the Christian and Missionary Alliance

Vol. XIVB
of the
"CHRIST IN THE BIBLE" Series

CHRISTIAN PUBLICATIONS, Inc.
Third and Reily Streets
Harrisburg, Pa.

The Mark of [logo] vibrant faith

EST. 1886

(Printed in the United States of America)

CONTENTS

I. The Son of Man 9

II. The Holy Child 21

III. The Baptism of Jesus 34

IV. The Temptation of the Son of Man 47

V. The First Message of the Son of Man 62

VI. The Son of Man and the Sinner 77

VII. The Son of Man and the Home 90

VIII. The Son of Man and the First Disciples 101

IX. The Parables of Divine Mercy.. 113

X. The Parables of Divine Mercy (Continued) 131

XI. The Parables of Human Destiny 148

XII. The Parables of Human Destiny (Continued) 163

XIII. The Son of Man and Sickness .. 175

XIV. The Sufferings of the Son of Man 184

XV. The Son of Man in His Resurrection Life 195

XVI. The Parting Scenes 204

CHAPTER I.

THE SON OF MAN.

"Behold the Man" (John xix. 5).

THE Gospel of Luke is the picture of the Son of man. The very fact that it begins with a preface is significant. The other Gospels have no preface, but immediately introduce us to the very heart of the subject. Luke presents to us the human medium through which this revelation of the Master comes. It is no disparagement to inspiration to recognize the coloring of the earthly medium through which the light is communicated. Luke tells us of his "perfect understanding" of all things of which he writes and leaves us to conclude that, with his trained mind, he has given the most thorough and painstaking inquiry into every fact and question that has come to him, and that while the Holy Ghost has guided and controlled, at the same time the instrument has been used with the fullest recognition of all his special qualifications for the task assumed.

The first two chapters of Luke contain a number of testimonies to our Lord, especially in connection with His birth, which have not been recorded by any other evangelist.

THE ANNOUNCEMENT OF THE BIRTH OF JOHN.

The first of these is the announcement to Zechariah of the birth of John, the great Forerunner. The revelation comes to him from the angel Gabriel as he is ministering in the holy place in the due course of his priesthood. The messenger informs him that his prayer is heard and that God is about to give a son to him and his godly partner after long delay, and when, in the course of human events, such a blessing had become improbable. Zechariah receives the message with astonishment and doubt, and asks for a sign to confirm his hesitating faith. The angel gives him a sign which is at once a reproof to his unbelief and a prop to his faith. He tells him that he shall be dumb until the prophecy shall have been fulfilled.

There was extraordinary significance in this sign. It was not merely a miraculous testimony of the prophecy just given, but it was a striking symbol of a still greater fact.

Zechariah represented the priesthood of Israel, and his unbelief was just a type of the unbelief of the nation in the coming Messiah, and the judgment upon that priesthood for its unbelief. Israel was to be silenced as the messenger of God because she had failed to be true to her divine commission and to believe the Gospel of which she had been made the trustee, and God was to put her aside and choose instead a new body of inspired messengers. And so God will silence every voice that fails to honor His well-beloved Son, and honor every voice that bears witness to Jesus Christ.

This is in keeping with Luke's special ministry to portray the Saviour and His wider relation to the Gentiles rather than to Israel. With the ministry of Zechariah, and John, his distinguished son, the voice of Israel was to cease and the Church of God was to come instead.

THE ANNUNCIATION.

The Annunciation to Mary is in the same spirit. The angel Gabriel appears to her in the seclusion of her modest life, and, bear-

ing to her the greeting of heaven upon the
high honor that was to be bestowed upon
her, he announces the birth to her of a divine Son. But the name he gives Him is
the name which belongs to sinners of every
race, Jesus. "Thou shalt call His name
Jesus." Then are added the majestic words
which tell of His deity as "the Son of the
Highest," and His heirship to David's
throne, and His kingdom "which shall have
no end." Her modest question, "How shall
this be?" was not a word of doubt, but simply of inquiry, and as the answer comes
telling her how the Holy Ghost shall accomplish this stupendous and holy miracle, she
believes and answers, "Behold the handmaid
of the Lord; be it unto me according to thy
word."

Here again we see the human element in
our great redemption. There must be a co-
operation of some believing soul before even
the Son of God could become incarnate.
While we guard against the exaggerations
and blasphemies of the Church of Rome in
giving to her equal worship and homage
with God, at the same time let us not with-
hold from her the veneration and love which
God intended that all ages should accord to

that one woman whose consecration and faith rolled back the curse which the sin and folly of another woman had brought upon the human race.

The visit of Mary to her cousin Elizabeth is the next incident in this chain of testimony. It would seem that she hastened to her cousin in the hill country of Judea as soon as the angel's strange message had been fully realized. She needed the sympathy of a true sister in this tremendous crisis, and so the two women met without previous knowledge by any earthly means of their several conditions. How perfectly natural as well as supernatural is the narrative of this meeting. Taught by the Holy Ghost, Elizabeth pours out in inspired language her greeting to the mother of her Lord; tells of her own strange joy and coming motherhood, and adds the benediction, "Blessed is she that believed, for there shall be a performance of those things which were told her from the Lord."

THE MAGNIFICAT.

The song of Mary which follows rises to a higher plane. It is Jewish throughout, breathing the very essence of the old cove-

nant and the spirit of the ancient prophets;
but it goes back beyond Moses to Abraham, and thus rises to that lofty plane from
which the Apostle Paul ever grasped the
Gospel plan of salvation. But while a Hebrew psalm, Mary's *Magnificat* is in perfect
keeping with Luke's purpose to reveal the
Saviour to the Gentiles. As some one has
well said, it is the swan song of Judaism,
the dying dirge of the old dispensation.
Mary reaches the very highest point of Hebrew poetry and lofty vision, and then she
stands aside lost in the light of her greater
Son as the chorus of redemption begins with
its world-wide and eternal refrain.

THE PROMISED FULFILMENT.

The Birth of John and the Testimony of
Zechariah. At length the promise of the
Forerunner is fulfilled and a child is born to
aged Zechariah and Elizabeth. Her cousins
and neighbors gather to hail the event with
rejoicing, and on the appointed day they
meet to circumcise the child, and they call
him Zechariah, after his father. But the
mother forbids and appeals to the father,
and he in turn declares on the writing tab-
let, "His name is John." His long silence is

broken, and, filled with the Holy Ghost, he
begins to praise God and utters his sublime
testimony not only to John, but to Jesus
(Luke i. 68-79).

This is the glorious Gospel of salvation.
First is the keynote of the incarnation. "He
hath visited His people." Next comes the
echo of the cross. "He hath redeemed His
people." Then we have the fulness of the
great salvation which He is about to reveal.
"That He would grant unto us that we, being delivered out of the hand of our enemies, might serve Him without fear in holiness and righteousness before Him all the
days of our life." This is the Gospel in all
its fulness.

Then follows the special introduction of
John's ministry. "Thou shalt be called the
prophet of the Highest, for thou shalt go
before the face of the Lord to prepare His
way." Next his special ministry of repentance and remission of sins is specified. "To
give knowledge of salvation unto His people by the remission of their sins through
the tender mercy of our God." Then the
vision expands into the larger fulness of
the perfect day, of which this was but the
dawning. "The dayspring from on high

hath visited us to give light to them that
sit in darkness and in the shadow of death,
to guide our feet into the way of peace."

GOOD TIDINGS.

The message of the angels to the shepherds of Bethlehem (chap. ii. 1-20). Here
again the keynote is loftier and larger than
in the other Gospels. Matthew opens with
the question, "Where is He that is born
King of the Jews?" but the message of the
angels to the shepherds is, "Unto you is
born to-day in the city of David a Saviour
which is Christ, the Lord." The spirit of
the message is joy and gladness. The very
word the angels use is the sweet word that
has passed into all Christian speech, the
Gospel. "I bring you good tidings"; that
is, I bring you the Gospel. The keynote of
their message is gladness and great joy, and
it is no longer the joy of a little exclusive
company, but "I bring you good tidings of
great joy which shall be to all people." And
then the song with which this glorious evangel is climaxed prolongs the notes in a still
grander refrain: "Glory to God in the highest, on earth peace, good will toward men."
How perfectly this fits into the scene

which follows. "They found Mary and Joseph and the Babe lying in a manger." This is the inauguration of the world's redemption. Not in palace halls and amid pageants of earthly grandeur, not with princes leading the inaugural procession, but with a company of shepherds at their nightly task as the first witnesses. And the Saviour Himself is introduced with a lowliness and poverty in keeping with the calling of the shepherds and the condition of the sinful world to which He has come. Thus the story of salvation is begun and the Saviour of sinners enters upon the stage of human suffering as our Brother and our Kinsman Redeemer.

THE TESTIMONY OF SIMEON AND ANNA.

One more testimony completes this striking chain. (Luke ii. 2-38.) The eighth day of our Saviour's life brings His circumcision, followed soon after by His presentation in the temple. How natural, yet supernatural again, is the whole scene. Without notice or invitation cards, Simeon and Anna meet at the right moment by the intuition of the Holy Spirit. The whole circumstances are very touching and intensely human. The offering which Mary and Joseph bring is the offering presented

only by the very poorest of the people, a
pair of turtle doves, or two young pigeons.
But as the little Babe is presented and the
aged priest receives him in his arms, the
whole scene is transfigured, and that sublime testimony which fittingly closes this
series of witnesses to the birth of Christ
flows from his lips. Taking the infant Jesus
in his arms, how truly he can say, "Mine
eyes have seen Thy salvation." What a beautiful picture of faith, not only accepting but
embracing the Lord! But the salvation
which He has prepared is as wide as the
world "which Thou hast prepared before the
face of all people." He adds, "A light to
lighten the Gentiles, and the glory of Thy
people Israel." Here is the Gospel for both
Jew and Gentile. Here is the watchword of
the missionary crusade and the promise of
the Chosen People's final restoration. And
as the scene closes he turns to Mary and
adds a message more personal to her, and
yet as true for every one of us, "This Child
is set for the fall and rising again of many
in Israel, and for a sign that shall be spoken
against, that the thoughts of many hearts
may be revealed; yea, a sword shall pierce
through thine own soul also."

The shadow of the cross is not only to fall upon Him, but upon her, and yes, upon all that receive Him. They must fall before they can rise. They must die before they can live. They must get down to nothingness before they can rise to holiness and heaven.

Simeon's testimony was followed by that of Anna, who, womanlike, went out to tell the joyful news to those who waited for redemption in Jerusalem.

Thus dawned the glorious light of the Sun of righteousness and the Saviour of the world. Shall we catch the spirit of these opening scenes in the beautiful Gospel of Luke? Shall we hear the blessed "Fear not" which is its very keynote, and enter into the gladness of the good tidings which it brings? Shall we accept it not merely as our heritage of blessing, but our trust to pass on to all the world? And shall we fully recognize with deeper, truer love the human Christ, the Son of man, the Kinsman Redeemer, who is bone of our bone, flesh of our flesh and heart of our heart, and go forth to walk in closer fellowship with His great human heart and constant sympathy?

2

"We may not climb the heavenly steeps
   To bring the Lord Christ down;
In vain we search the lowest depths,
   For Him no depths can drown.

"But warm, sweet, tender, even yet
   A present help is He;
And faith has still its Olivet
   And love its Galilee.

"The healing of His seamless robe
   Is by our beds of pain;
We touch Him in life's throng and press
   And we are whole again."

Chapter II.

THE HOLY CHILD.

"And the Child grew and waxed strong in spirit, filled with wisdom, and the grace of God was upon Him" (Luke ii. 40).

"And Jesus increased in wisdom and stature and in favor with God and man" (Luke ii. 52).

THE CHILDHOOD OF CHRIST.

LUKE lingers over the human picture and the home life of our blessed Lord. "The Child grew." How perfectly natural this is! How different from the story of the first creation! Adam sprang to life full grown and fell. The second Adam began as a helpless babe and traversed every step of the pilgrimage of man from the cradle to the grave, and He has lifted up and redeemed the race.

There is a clear suggestion here of the threefold humanity of our Lord, and the perfectly natural development of each part.

HIS PHYSICAL LIFE.

"The Child grew." That is the first thing for a child to do. The perfect physical development and health of your child should take precedence of all other things. Too often the body is stunted and depressed

by over-ambitious parents in pushing the
mere intellectual culture of their children.
Our Lord Jesus had a sound physical life,
and all through His earthly existence we
find Him giving proper care to His body,
and free from asceticism and extremes of
every kind so that He even received the reproach from His enemies, "The Son of man
came eating and drinking." While physical
culture may be carried to an extreme, and no
doubt is in many modern schools, yet, a sound
mind in a sound body is in perfect keeping
with the principles of the common sense religion which Christ has taught us.

HIS SPIRITUAL LIFE.

Spiritual culture took the second place in
the development of Jesus. It came before all
educational processes for mere mental training. "He waxed strong in spirit." The spirit
is our higher nature including conscience with
its instinctive knowledge of right and wrong,
and the faculty to know God, to pray to Him,
to love Him and to obey Him. All this was
carefully trained by the pious mother of our
blessed Lord, and gradually He drank in from
her lofty spirit those higher inspirations which
formed the strength of her holy character.

"FILLED WITH WISDOM."

This embraces the educational processes through which His mind was trained. But there was more than the mere acquisition of knowledge. His was a practical education which turned mere knowledge into wisdom, the power to utilize knowledge and bring things to pass. Too much of our modern education lacks this. The brain is crammed, the memory stored with facts and theories which are soon forgotten, and have little value as actual forces in the formation of character or the accomplishment of the work of life.

"THE GRACE OF GOD WAS UPON HIM."

The influence behind all, and over all His early life was the recognition of God and the spirit of piety. Of course, such a mother as Mary could not bring up her child in any other way. Happy for all children if their parents would recognize the capacity of even the youngest child to spiritual influences. It is but a short step to heaven from the instincts of the youngest child, and through the medium of a loving and holy mother it is not hard to mold the earliest conceptions and thoughts of life in a heavenly pattern.

The synagogue at Nazareth no doubt was furnished like Hebrew synagogues with the regular scrolls containing the Sacred Volume, and also a plan of the Tabernacle and Temple, and once every day, and three times on Sabbath it was customary for pious households to gather for the worship of God. Under all these influences the childhood of Jesus developed, and His earnest spirit reached out after sacred truth in many a longing and perhaps many a question which led up to the next important incident in His young life, when the opportunity came in the temple to satisfy the deep desires and questionings which had already reached out beyond the light which even His mother was able to give.

What a beautiful example for the Christian parent and the Christian child Luke has given us in this simple story of the "Holy Child Jesus"!

THE BOYHOOD OF CHRIST.

(Luke ii. 41-51.)

The age of twelve is a kind of turning point in the life of every boy, a narrow strait leading out from the harbor of childhood into the larger ocean of early manhood.

How important to have a wise pilot to
guide the little ship through the dangerous
passage. It is then that the boy begins to
awake to all the powers and possibilities of
his being, and the world grows bigger to
his eyes in response to that other world of
inward consciousness, which he finds within his soul. It was at that time that the
Hebrew law provided for the bringing of
Jewish boys into the full recognition of their
responsibilities as "sons of the law." For
this purpose Jesus was taken by His parents
to Jerusalem to the Passover in His twelfth
year. Every year they had faithfully gone
up since His birth, but now He accom-
panies them for the first time. It was a
long, weary journey, and even to-day on
the strongest and swiftest of beasts of burden it takes two and a half days from Nazareth to Jerusalem.

ON THE WAY TO JERUSALEM.

The author of Ben Hur has given us an
imaginary picture of that little caravan. Joseph, a man of middle age, is leading the
party on foot; Mary, the modest mother,
still a young woman, is seated on the don-
key following close behind, and walking

alongside is a lad of twelve, perhaps with a
face like that exquisite picture given us by
Hoffman, thoughtful, pure and strangely
earnest, the brow covered by the usual white
handkerchief of the Bedouin, the corner
turned in over the forehead, a white tunic
covering His graceful frame below the
knees, and His feet shod with rough sandals,
while He holds in His hand a long staff
higher than His own stature.

At length they reach the city, crowded at
this time in the early Spring with a popula-
tion six times its ordinary size, and with
others they camp out on the hillsides round
about and prepare for the solemn services
of the Passover.

PREPARATION FOR THE PASSOVER.

With what intense interest He must have
watched them as they selected the lamb and
kept it apart for three days, typical of the
three years of the Messiah's earthly ministry,
and then on the fourth day offered up its life
at the appointed hour with solemn sacrificial
services, sprinkling its blood upon the door-
posts and then roasting its flesh for the Paschal
meal. The very form in which it was prepared
was significant. Two skewers were passed

through the lamb crosswise, and thus it was hung above the fire and slowly roasted, presenting the perfect symbol of His own cross. At the appointed time the Passover meal began with the purging out of every speck of leaven. Then followed the cup of wine, the unleavened bread, the bitter herbs and the flesh of the lamb.

At a certain point in the feast some child in the household would ask the question, "What meaneth this service?" No doubt on this occasion it would be the lad Jesus Himself, and from His lips what intense pathos that question had. In reply Joseph would tell the story of that night in ancient Egypt when the destroying angel passed by and the sprinkled blood saved Israel's first born from the curse of sin. And doubtless he would also tell of the coming Messiah in whom all this was to be fulfilled, and Mary's face and falling tears would bear witness to how much it meant for her and her precious child.

WITH THE DOCTORS OF THE LAW.

Influences such as these naturally worked up His mind to the most intense interest in the scenes that were all around Him, and the services of that wondrous temple which for the

first time He beheld.   Little wonder that He
soon found His way to the class room where
aged Hillel and other doctors of the law were
discussing the deep questions of their national
faith.   As the hours flew by He took no note
of time, but became intensely absorbed in
hearing and asking questions, while they in
turn were as much amazed at the wonderful
answers which he often gave.

"HOW IS IT THAT YE SOUGHT ME?"

Hours passed into days and already Joseph
and Mary had turned homeward with the
large caravan containing many of the kinsfolk.
It was not until the evening she discovered
that her precious child was missing.   "A lost
child!"   How the words stir our hearts and
set in motion the bells of the town, the wires of
the telephone and the hearts of anxious mothers.   But, oh, what a child was this that was
lost that day!   One can faintly imagine the
suspense and anguish of Mary's heart as they
eagerly retraced their steps and sought for
Him through all the city.   Three days of anx-
iety and despair passed before at length they
found Him still absorbed in the Bible class of
the temple.   One can almost imagine the ac-
cents with which she cried as she embraced

Him, "Son, why hast thou dealt thus with us? Behold, Thy father and I have sought Thee sorrowing." But what elocution or rhetoric can give full weight to the wondrous answer that came so simply and spontaneously from His lips, "How is it that ye sought Me? Wist ye not that I must be about My Father's business?"

Just one glimpse this incident gives us of all those early years. But, oh, how much it tells of the deep unfolding of His mind and heart, and the perfectly human yet superhuman development of the character of Jesus. How beautiful to think that this blessed Christ is the Saviour and Friend of every boy and girl. Edmund of Canterbury tells how once in a dream, when a lad of twelve, He met a beautiful boy of the same age, and followed him long, charmed with His face and conversation. As he seemed about to leave him he said, "Oh, that I could be with you always." And the Boy turned and said, "Why, I am with you always. When you sit at your class in school, lo, I am there helping you. When you lie down upon your bed at home, I am there protecting you. In your work and in your prayer I am ever with you." And Edmund looked up and saw the name of Jesus upon His brow.

And the Boy said, "Just whisper this name and you will always find Me by your side."

Oh, boys and girls, this blessed Christ is yours. Whatever your age, He was once just as old and just as young. Whatever your circumstances He was there, and if you, too, will breathe that sweet name you will hear a gentle voice reply, "Lo, I am with you alway, even unto the end of the world."

And for us men and women of larger growth the message of the holy Child is just as timely. Your Father's business, are you about it? Is your life as earnest and as consecrated as His? Is there a *"must"* controlling and constraining every power of your being and every moment of your existence for highest service and holiest usefulness? A simple workman whose daily toil was inscribed with "Holiness unto the Lord," was once asked what his business was, and his answer deserves to be written over every shop and factory and office and calling, "My business is to serve the Lord, but I make shoes for a living." Beloved, are you about your Father's business?

No time for trifling in this life of mine,
  Not this the path the blessed Master trod;
But strenuous toil, each hour and power employed
    Always and all for God.

HIS EARLY MANHOOD.

"And He went down with them and came to Nazareth and was subject unto them" (Luke ii. 51). This is all we know about eighteen long years of the Master's life. But how much it embraces.

SUBJECTION.

This is just another word for discipline. Our excessive liberty has degenerated into license and we are growing weary of God's old-fashioned methods of training. But it is still true, as has been wisely and wittily said, "One of life's chief missions is not foreign missions nor home missions, but submission." If we are not willing to learn our lesson at home we shall have to have it taught us in harder fashion between the millstones of life's trials. No character can be strong without learning to yield, to suffer, and to obey.

TOIL.

The sentence passed upon the first Adam, "In the sweat of thy brow," must be literally fulfilled by the second Adam, and by all His followers who expect to pass with Him first through the downward progression of humiliation and suffering, and then through His exal-

tation and glory. A luxurious age is trying
to get away from the law of labor. But to do
this we must leave our Lord behind us. Idle-
ness is the twin brother of crime, and some
one has truly said of toil,

"Blest toil, if thou were cursed of God,
What must His blessing be!"

THE SHADOW OF THE CROSS.

Holman Hunt has left us the vivid painting
of the toiling Christ returning at sunset from
His carpenter's bench and stretching His arms
horizontally in a momentary paroxysm of
weariness while the sun caught His figure and
threw His shadow across the opposite wall in
the form of the cross. Under that shadow
He always walked, and we should be willing
to walk with Him too. Probably their lot was
extremely poor. Possibly He was the bread-
winner of the family as the eldest if not the
only son, and if, as has been suggested, Joseph
had died during his childhood and left Him
with His mother leaning upon His care. The
wages of a carpenter would not exceed at the
very highest twenty-five cents a day, and the
hours were from sunrise to sunset. On this
pittance He supported His loved ones and lived
in a humble home which was half a cave, a

stranger to all the comforts of luxuries which a modern tradesman's family can enjoy.

Someone has told us of another beautiful dream in which he seemed to be standing just outside their cottage door at Nazareth with the carpenter's shop near by; and as he watched he saw a middle-aged man working at a carpenter's bench and a lad picking up the chips. And then a maiden came and called them into the cottage for their evening meal, and all they had was coarse bread and milk. Before they tasted, the Boy, with a face all beaming with love, looked toward the stranger at the door and said, "Why does the stranger stand outside? Let him come in and eat with us." Blessed Christ! Blessed heart of human tenderness and divine love! Oh, that our childhood, our manhood, and our latest years may be so linked with Thine and so filled with Thy gentle Spirit that we, too, shall leave behind us upon every path of life through which we pass some of the light which Thou hast left upon the home of Nazareth and the path of life.

Chapter III.

THE BAPTISM OF JESUS.

"Wherefore, in all things it behooved Him to be made like unto His brethren, that He might be a merciful and faithful High Priest in things pertaining to God, to make reconciliation for the sins of the people" (Heb. ii. 17).

IN no respect was the perfect humanity of Jesus Christ, and His entire identification with our fallen race more strikingly manifested than in His submission to the ordinance of baptism at the hands of John. That ordinance was an explicit confession on the part of those receiving it of their utter sinfulness, and their need of the divine forgiveness. And the act was a striking symbol of death and resurrection on the part of the subjects of baptism. It was an actual confession that they were so utterly guilty and lost that there was no hope of self-improvement, and they must therefore yield to the judgment of God and die, so far as every personal merit was concerned, and then be brought back to an entirely new life through the sovereign mercy and grace of God.

SIGNIFICANCE OF CHRIST'S BAPTISM.

The impropriety of Christ submitting to such baptism, in view of His personal innocence and utter freedom from all taint of sin, was so obvious to John the Baptist that he at first refused to allow the Lord to be baptized by him, and only consented because of Christ's insistence. Why then did our Lord insist on receiving a rite which was so explicit a confession of sin? The answer is very solemn and glorious. It was because He identified Himself with sinful men, and in symbol went down with them to the death which they deserved as He was afterwards to suffer that death in actual reality. No wonder that when He came forth from the waters of baptism the great Forerunner pointed to Him on the banks of the Jordan and cried, "Behold the Lamb of God, which taketh away the sin of the world!" His baptism had been a rehearsal of the cross and a type of the great atonement which He was afterwards to accomplish on Calvary.

SIGNIFICANCE OF OURS.

This is the deepest significance of the ordinance of baptism for us His disciples to-

3

day. As He went down with us to death
and took away our curse and sin, so we go
down with Him by baptism into death, and
become partakers of His atonement and redemption. Baptism is therefore not a symbol of cleansing, but of crucifixion; not of
self-improvement, but of self-effacement and
resurrection life in Him, our risen Head.
"Know ye not that so many of us as were
baptized into Jesus Christ were baptized
into His death, that like as Christ was
raised up from the dead by the glory of the
Father, even so, we also should walk in
newness of life."

Luke gives a fine touch to the human picture of our Lord's baptism by a single
phrase in the twenty-first verse of the third
chapter. "Now, when all the people were
baptized, it came to pass that Jesus also
being baptized, and praying, the heaven
was opened," etc. It was when all the people were baptized that He went into the
Jordan's flood unostentatiously just like any-
body else. Probably to the ordinary ob-
server there was nothing to distinguish
Him from the crowds of sinful men that
pressed into the waters, and but for the
special sign which had been given to John,

even he would not have recognized Him, for speaking of it himself he says, "I knew Him not." There was no parade of His importance. There was no halo around His brow. There was no proclamation of His divine condescension, but standing on the level of our lost humanity, going down with us into the common grave, which typified our just doom, "He was made in all things like unto His brethren that He might be a merciful and faithful High Priest in things pertaining to God, to make reconciliation for the sins of the people."

There is also another touch of humanness in Luke's narrative. It is found in the words "and praying." As He went down to His baptism He was in the attitude of a dependent man, having no strength of His own, and looking up to God for grace and blessing. There is nothing more comforting than the uniform attitude of the Lord Jesus Christ to that heavenly grace upon which we are so dependent through the open gates of prayer. He who might have commanded all the resources of the skies took the lowly position of a suppliant at the throne of grace, and still bends with us as we also come coupling His personality with our own as we say, "OUR Father, which art in heaven."

THE BAPTISM OF THE SPIRIT.

But the scene which followed gives a grander climax to this picture of the human Christ. "The heaven was opened and the Holy Ghost descended in a bodily shape like a dove upon Him; and a voice came from heaven which said, Thou art My beloved Son in whom I am well pleased." The baptism of Jesus Christ with the Holy Ghost marks an epoch in His earthly life. From this moment all His public ministry began and all His work was accomplished in dependence upon the Holy Ghost. He did not claim to work miracles through His essential Deity, but acknowledged, "If I, by the Spirit of God, cast out demons, no doubt the kingdom of God is come unto you." He did not meet the tempter in the wilderness in His own inherent strength, but "He was led up of the Spirit into the wilderness, to be tempted of the devil." And He went back from the conflict "in the power of the Spirit." He did not stand before the people as a great Teacher through His wisdom, but He stood up in the synagogue at Nazareth and declared, "The Spirit of the Lord is upon Me, because He hath anointed Me to preach the Gospel to the poor; He hath sent Me to heal the broken hearted; to preach deliverance to the captives; and recovering of sight to the blind; to set at liberty them that are bruised; to preach the acceptable year of the Lord." The Apostle John, in quoting His own words, says, "I do nothing of Myself, but as My Father hath taught Me I speak these things."

THE REAL HUMANITY OF CHRIST.

Is it not true that we have been accustomed to think of the Lord Jesus as having some special and individual advantage of us through His divine nature and perhaps to say "Christ could do that because He was the Son of God, but I cannot be expected to do such things"? Have we not failed to realize that while Christ was indeed the Son of God, and can never cease to be, yet when He came down as the Son of man to represent our race and to work out our salvation, He suspended the prerogatives and resources of His deity, and took the place of a dependent man, drawing all His strength from God through faith and prayer

even as we must do? How near this brings
Him to us, and how truly He could say, "If
I by the Spirit of God cast out demons, no
doubt the kingdom of God is come near
unto you." That is to say the same Spirit
that dwelt in Him is now given to us and
through Him we may share the same enduement of power from on high.

THE HOLY GHOST AND JESUS.

In receiving the baptism of the Holy
Ghost Jesus was our Forerunner. Let us bear
in mind that up to this time He had not
been without the Holy Spirit. He was born
of the Spirit, for had not the angel said to
Mary, "The Holy Ghost shall come upon
thee, and the power of the Highest shall
overshadow thee; therefore that holy thing
that shall be born of thee shall be called
the Son of God." In like manner we are
also born of the Spirit from the moment
of our conversion, and become the children
of God. But that day on the banks of the
Jordan something more than this came to
our Lord. The Holy Ghost as a person actually removed from the heavens and came
down to earth, and henceforth resided as a
distinct Person in union with the Son of

man. From this time forward there were
two persons united in the life and ministry
of Jesus Christ, the Holy Ghost and the
Lord Jesus, and all He said and did was in
the power of the Spirit. This is just what
happens to the consecrated believer when he
receives the baptism with the Holy Ghost.
He has been a child of God before. Born
of the Spirit he has had the Spirit with him.
But now the Holy Ghost comes to be in him,
so united to him that all his life henceforth
is accomplished in constant dependence
upon and fellowship with that divine Presence. It is as when the bride loses her personality, in a sense, in dependence upon
her husband. Down that aisle they walk
alone, but from that marriage altar they return no longer alone, but united. Henceforth her name is lost in his. Her support
is derived from him, or ought to be, and her
will is yielded to him. Something infinitely greater than this comes to pass when our
life passes out of the human into the divine, and we can truly say,

Once it was my working,
　His it hence shall be;
Once I tried to use Him,
　Now He uses me.

Oh, beloved, if the Lord Jesus did not presume to begin His public ministry or perform a single service as our Teacher and Example until He received the Holy Ghost, what right have we to go forth in our self-sufficiency and attempt to minister at the altar of Christian service until we be endued with power from on high?

HIS HUMAN PEDIGREE.

In striking testimony to the perfect humanness of all this scene is the fact that Luke introduces the genealogy of the Lord Jesus at this very point. This genealogy, unlike that in Matthew, is traced back, not to Abraham, but to Adam. "Which was the son of Adam, which was the son of God," is the sublime climax of this long list of names which links the blessed Jesus with our fallen race. His pedigree therefore is not that of a Jew, but of a man; not the descendant of Abraham, but the son of Adam. Well may the apostle say, "Verily, He took not on Him the nature of angels, but He took on Him the seed of Abraham."

The genealogical line given us by Luke differs in all its important links from that

of Matthew, and we must accept the expla-
nation and hypothesis that it is given in the
line of Mary, while Matthew's is traced in
the line of Joseph. All that is necessary to
make this plain is simply to interpret, as was
customary among the Hebrews, the word
"son" in verse 23 as "son-in-law."

How may we follow our blessed Forerunner in thus receiving the baptism of the
Spirit?

THE BAPTISM OF THE SPIRIT A DEATH.

1. Like Him let us yield ourselves to
death. This just stands for that act of definite surrender and consecration in which
every marked spiritual crisis must begin. It
comes to each one of us differently, but it
accomplishes the same result in each case.
It searches our hearts to their inmost
depths. It brings to light each hidden sin
and cherished idol, and especially all the
depths of our self-sufficiency and self-will,
and it lays us broken, helpless and wholly
yielded at the feet of sovereign grace. The
deeper the death, the higher will be the life
to which it leads. The more complete the
surrender and the separation, the more glorious will be the blessing. Let us not be

afraid to be thoroughly honest and inexor-
ably true to the life the Spirit brings. Let
us give up self as well as sin, and say as
utterly as the great apostle could say, "I
have been crucified with Christ, nevertheless
I live, yet not I, but Christ liveth in me."

Usually we shall find that there is some
special form of self and sin to which the
heart is clinging, some hidden idol in which
all the roots and tendrils of the carnal heart
have concentrated their strength. It is gen-
erally the last thing we are willing to see
and let go. And therefore consecration often hinges upon one special decision or surrender. But it is more than a negative surrender. It is a positive accepting of and entering into all the will of God for us. It is
an infinite privilege to be permitted to make
such a consecration and to receive such a
blessing. The consecration of Jesus Christ
that day was not merely a surrender to
death, but an acceptance of all His Father's
will. Let us therefore come not merely to
give up everything, but to receive infinitely
more. When we kneel at the altar of sacrifice there is Another who kneels with us,
and just as fully as we give ourselves to
Him He gives Himself to us, and His own

glorious promise is, "For their sakes I con-
secrate Myself that they may be truly consecrated."

NECESSITY OF FAITH.

2. Therefore faith is as essential as consecration in receiving the baptism of the Holy
Ghost. We must believe that God accepts
us just as surely as we have surrendered
ourselves to Him. We must take as well as
give. We must be fully assured that the
Father receives us in His beloved Son, and
says of us as truly as of Him, "In thee I
am well pleased." We must recognize the
Holy Spirit as actually coming to us, and
henceforth taking up His abode within us;
and we must begin to treat Him as if He
were our indwelling Guest, and our ever-
abiding Comforter and Guide. We must
think of God as no longer in some distant
heaven, but actually within us, and the
throne of grace as in our very hearts where
we may pray with confidence and dwell in
communion in the "Holiest of All." We
must go forth expecting His presence, His
power, His response to our every cry, and
His all-sufficiency for our every need. Thus
walking in the Spirit we too shall find that

our life has been translated and transfigured from the earthly to the heavenly, from
the human to the divine, from our endeavor
to God's best.

Oh, what a privilege, what an honor,
what a boundless possibility all this opens
up to us weak and worthless children of
Adam's fallen race! Truly since that morning on Jordan's strand, the heaven is open
and the kingdom of God has come near to
us! Let us recognize it. Let us receive
it and let us hear the voice of ancient prophecy inviting us, "Oh, house of Jacob, come
ye, and let us walk in the light of the
Lord."

CHAPTER IV.

THE TEMPTATION OF THE SON OF MAN.

"He was in all points tempted like as we are, yet without sin" (Heb. iv. 15).

"In that He Himself hath suffered being tempted, He is able to succour them that are tempted" (Heb. ii. 18).

THE baptism of the Holy Ghost is not given to us primarily as an enduement of power for service. This is one of the mistaken teachings that are abroad to-day. Undoubtedly power for service is one result of this blessing, but it is primarily given to us for personal character and holiness; for what we are to be rather than what we are to do and say. This is surely demonstrated by the fact that, after receiving the baptism of the Spirit, our Lord— our Example and Forerunner—did not immediately begin His public ministry, but first went alone for a personal conflict with the adversary, and for the testing and establishing of His own personal victory and righteousness. The forty days of Christ's temptation mean a good deal more than forty days in the experience of His disciples and cover the whole experience of our

Christian life in the conflict with sin and
Satan. Indeed, the supreme factor in our
service is personal character and experience.
It is only the men and women who have
been there themselves who can lead others
through the conflict and into the victory.

THE FACT OF TEMPTATION.

The fact that Jesus Christ was tempted is
the most emphatic proof of His actual humanity. It was in our nature that He was
tempted, for "God cannot be tempted with
evil, neither tempteth He any man." It
was as the second Adam, and the representative of our struggling race that the Lord
Jesus entered the lists that day with the
great adversary and proved that no mortal
again need ever despair. Temptation is
still a fact in every human life. But, it is
also true, "there hath no temptation taken
you, but such as is common to man, but
God is faithful who will not suffer you to
be tempted above that ye are able, but will
with the temptation also make a way of escape that ye may be able to bear it."

THE AGENT IN THE TEMPTATION.

The agent in the temptation is called the

devil. The Bible has a way of calling
things by their right names which we would
be wise to follow. The devil has achieved
no greater triumph than to succeed in hid-
ing his identity from this advanced age. If
a brigand could only succeed in posing as
one of a tourist party whom he intended to
rob, he would have little difficulty in carry-
ing out his plans. This is just what Satan
has attempted and accomplished in many
quarters to-day, and while men are laughing
at the idea of a devil he is playing off his
disguise and leading men captive at his will.
Doubtless he came to Christ as he still
comes to us, not in some open and repulsive form, but in deep disguise and probably by such subtle suggestions as could
easily be mistaken for the promptings of
His own mind.

THE CIRCUMSTANCES OF THE TEMPTATION.

The first great test came to man in a paradise of beauty and delight, but it ended in
a tragedy. The second came in the desolate wilderness, but it led up to Paradise
restored. The adversary chooses his battle-
field with wise discrimination. He came to
Christ when His body was enfeebled with

long fasting, and His spirit perhaps clouded
with the gloomy surroundings of His situation. He will always attack us at our worst.
When the frame is worn with sickness, the
body racked with pain, and the spirit depressed with discouragement and sorrow,
then look out for the crafty and cruel adversary.

THE TIME OF THE TEMPTATION.

It was after a great blessing and before
a great service. Jesus had just stood at the
open heaven and received the baptism of the
Holy Ghost, and the message of His Father, "This is My beloved Son, in whom I
am well pleased." And He was about to
begin His great life, and His mighty assault
upon Satan's kingdom. Therefore all the
forces of hell were roused against Him. It
was when David was crowned king in He-
bron that "the Philistines came to seek
for David." An old writer has said, "So
long as Jesus was occupied with the chips
of the carpenter shop, the devil paid little
attention to Him; but when He came forth
in the power of the Spirit to conquer him,
then the gauge of battle was drawn." Let
us look out for danger in the hour of spir-

itual elevation and glorious blessing, and
let us especially be prepared for the wiles of
the enemy when we are planning some high
service for God and our fellow men.

THE PURPOSE OF THE TEMPTATION.

Why was Jesus tempted of the devil?
Why is temptation permitted to come to
any man? Why does not God with one
lightning stroke destroy our cruel foe and
clear our way from every adversary and
obstacle?

If two young men were placed in a position of responsibility and trust, and the
one permitted every opportunity to be dis-
honest, and the other so hedged about that
all graft and dishonesty were made impossible, and both came forth at the end of their
period of probation with an irreproachable
record, which would have the higher moral
standing? Surely, the one that had been
tested in the face of temptation. The moral
character of the other would still be a matter of absolute uncertainty. Therefore it
was necessary that the human race should
be tested in the first creation, and it is still
necessary, in order to the development and
confirmation of character, that we should

pass through the ordeal of the tempter.
"Count it all joy," therefore, the apostle
says, "when ye fall in with divers temptations, knowing that the trying of your faith
worketh patience; but let patience have her
perfect work, that ye may be perfect and
entire, wanting nothing." All the more was
this necessary in the Master's case, because
His righteousness was not for Himself
alone, but was to be imputed to all His followers as the ground of their acceptance,
and it must be proved even in the face of
the gates of hell to be without a flaw. Fur-
thermore this conflict was a great representative battle in behalf of the race. It was
the decisive conflict of human history and
destiny. It was the second Adam taking
up the issue where the first had failed, and
winning back all that he had lost. It was
as necessary for Christ to stand victorious
in the wilderness as it was for Him without
a murmur to lay down His life upon the
cross. Both were vicarious offerings; the
one the offering of His righteousness; the
other of His life; and by both He has conquered hell and opened heaven to all believers.

THE METHOD AND PROCESS OF THE TEMPTA-
TION.

In many respects it was the very counterpart of the first great conflict in Eden.

The first attack was made upon the faith
of our Lord. "If Thou be the Son of God,"
the devil sneered; as much as to say, "You
the Son of God! Well, did I ever hear anything so absurd! The Son of God left by
His Father in this desolate wilderness, exposed to wild beasts and starving for
bread? Why, You are deluded. You must
be insane. Come, let us dispel this dream;
or, if You be the Son of God, let us have
some proof of it." And so the devil dared
the Lord to prove His character and claim.
Remember the subject of this temptation
was a real man with a mind as liable to discouragement, despondency, and the depres-
sion that comes from physical weakness as
yours and mine. Remember also that it is
your faith that the enemy assails and discouragement is the usual gateway to doubt
and unbelief Your worst faults and falls
are not so important to the great enemy of
your soul as the use which he intends to
make of them in crushing your spirit and destroying your confidence. Remember,

therefore, the stirring message of One who Himself was sorely tempted, "Whom resist steadfast in the faith, knowing that the same afflictions are accomplished in your brethren that are in the world." Remember, also, the words of another victorious soldier of the cross, "Above all, taking the shield of faith whereby ye shall be able to quench all the fiery darts of the wicked." "Cast not away therefore your confidence which hath great recompense of reward."

THE ATTACK UPON HIS PHYSICAL NATURE.

The second assault was upon His body and His physical appetites and desires. "Command that these stones shall be made bread." And so the first experiences of temptation are often through our physical nature, or our temporal circumstances. How often he comes to us through sickness and the choice is between his prescription and the Lord's help. How blessed to remember at such a time the Master's answer to the enemy, "Man shall not live by bread alone, but by every word that proceedeth out of the mouth of God." There is life in God for our bodies as well as for our spirits, and it were better even not to live than to live by the devil's help. How often the temptation comes through financial pressure. One of his fallacies is to say, "You must have a living and therefore you must do something to help yourself in this emergency." It is not always true that we must have a living. There came a time when the men of Babylon dared to say, "If it be so our God is able to deliver us, but if not, we will not worship the image which thou hast set up."

THE ATTACK UPON HIS AMBITION.

The next attack was upon His ambition. In some way the glory of earthly power was brought before Him in a moment and the possibility of His attaining it, if only He would put Himself under the direction of the arch fiend. Satan was the first political boss, and ever since he has been trying to make men his dupes. Oh, how many have sold their souls for power, ambition or graft! Doubtless in the case of our Lord he made it all appear beautiful and beneficent and pointed out, perhaps, the splendid use He could make of such power in bringing to an end the wrongs of His people, the cruel oppressions of earth's tyrants, and the manifold evils of humanity. But again Christ refused the tempting bribe simply because He would not take anything from Satan. Just as He would not have the devil's bread or the devil's medicine, He would not have the devil's crown, and the day came when from the Father He received a mightier dominion and could say without any thanks to the devil, "All power is given unto Me in heaven and in earth."

AN APPEAL TO SPIRITUAL PRIDE.

The climax was an appeal to His spiritual pride. The devil first attacked His body, next His soul, and finally His spirit. "Cast Thyself down," he cried, "from this lofty pinnacle of the temple, and God will work such a miracle for Your deliverance that the world will immediately flock to Your feet and hail You as its deliverer and its God." And then he began to quote some Scripture, but again Jesus met him word for word with the same weapon that he had used, "It is written again, Thou shalt not tempt the Lord thy God." The principle of the temptation, and the principle of the victory was the same as in the other assault. He refused to take Himself out of the place of a real man. He refused to turn aside from the

will of His Father and even work a miracle
to save Himself. Had He done so it would
have been the rejection of the cross and the
renouncing of the pathway of lowly humanity and suffering through which He was to
redeem the race. As a man He had gone
into that place of trial, and there He should
remain until deliverance came to Him not
through His own rash act, but through His
Father's loving hand. How perfect the picture of humanity. How truly "He was
tempted in all points like as we are, yet
without sin."

THE SECRET OF VICTORY.

The Word was His weapon. "It is written," was the sword of the Spirit which
again and again He wielded with such re-
sistless power. We cannot hope to stand in
the evil day unless we know our Bibles and
are taught by the Spirit how to use them.
The remarkable fact about His use of the
Bible was that most of His quotations were
taken from the book of Deuteronomy, the
very book which the devil and higher critics
have always tried to depreciate and discred-
it. Jesus took the very weakest of all His
weapons and used it to crush the serpent's
head.

THE HOLY SPIRIT.

"He was led of the Spirit into the wilderness," and He went forth in the power of the Spirit. "When the enemy shall come in like a flood, the Spirit of the Lord shall lift up a standard against him." It is only as we walk in the Spirit and follow Him closely that we can expect to overcome that crafty foe whose wisdom is too deep for us alone.

DEVOTION TO THE WILL OF GOD.

The deepest secret of Christ's triumph was His devotion to the will of God. "I must be about My Father's business," was the keynote of His life. He sought nothing for Himself. He would accept nothing for Himself. Nothing could tempt Him from the path of suffering to which He had given Himself in obedience to His Father's will, and this was the sheet anchor of His safety. This is that breast-plate of righteousness wherewith we shall be armed against the great enemy. It is a great and profound truth that Jesus Christ won His victory over Satan and won our redemption, not by brilliant wisdom, or superhuman power, but by simple righteousness. It was a moral triumph. Had He for a moment failed, our redemption had been lost, and He and we together perished in the ruin. Oh, beloved, remember the mightiest thing in your life is to be right and to do right at any cost. Against such a purpose the gates of hell cannot prevail.

THE RESULTS OF THE TEMPTATION.

"Jesus went forth in the power of the Spirit." He was stronger for the battle. And so shall we be. Every victory won imparts to you the strength that you have taken from your conquered foe. And by and by there shall be added the crown of recompense and the eternal reward which God is preparing not only for those that have worked for souls, but for those that have stood true in the evil day. "Blessed is the man that endureth temptation, for when he is tried he shall receive the crown of life which the Lord hath promised to them that love Him."

CHRIST'S FELLOWSHIP WITH US IN TEMPTATION.

This is the chief lesson of all this story. True to Luke's great purpose, the Son of man appears in the conflict of the wilderness as our Brother, our Champion and our great Example. For us He won back the victory that Adam, our first father, had so shamefully lost; and with us and in us still He overcomes as we follow His footsteps through temptation and trial. "In that He Himself suffered, being tempted, He is able also to succour them that are tempted." How tender and solemn His message to Peter, His tempted disciple, "Satan hath desired to have thee that he might sift thee as wheat, but I have prayed for thee that thy faith fail not. And when thou art converted strengthen thy brethren." And how faithfully Peter, in his turn, sought to fulfil this trust and help the tempted ones.

CONQUERORS THROUGH HIM.

The supreme lesson of all that we have been considering is that only in Christ can we hope to overcome our subtle foe. All who try this unequal conflict alone will surely fail. The sinner has ventured on the devil's territory and Satan has a right to every man who sins. There is One only who can set us free, and those who refuse His help must fall. The most fearful thing about the condition of ungodly men is that they are unable to give up sinning, and bound to fall under the power of the wicked one. "The Lord knoweth how to deliver the godly out of temptation and to reserve the ungodly unto the day of judgment to be punished." One of the saddest memories of the writer is the case of a man addicted to drink, who persistently refused to accept the Lord Jesus as his Saviour, declaring that he needed nothing better than his own manhood to give him the victory. In the last interview had with him he closed the conversation by saying, "I don't want your Jesus, I can save myself." A few months after this the awful tidings suddenly came that he had dropped dead in a drunken spree in one of the saloons in the city, and gone to his account with all his transgressions upon his head. Oh, tempted one, there is but One can succour and save you. The Son of man who conquered for you once, and is ready to conquer in you again.

> Fainting soldier of the Lord,
> Hear His sweet, inspiring word—
> I have conquered all thy foes;
> I have suffered all thy woes;
> Struggling soldier, trust in Me,
> I have overcome for thee.

Chapter V

THE FIRST MESSAGE OF THE SON
OF MAN.

"And Jesus returned in the power of the Spirit into Galilee: and there went out a fame of Him through all the region round about. And He taught in their synagogues, being glorified of all. And He came to Nazareth, where He had been brought up; and, as His custom was, He went into the synagogue on the Sabbath day, and stood up for to read" (Luke iv. 14-16).

THE remarkable incidents attending the birth, baptism and temptation of our Lord as recorded by Luke would naturally prepare us to expect some unusual opening of His public ministry. Nor are we disappointed. Like the frontispiece on the opening page of a volume, the incident of our text stands out in bold relief. How utterly human the picture is! Like all the other pictures which Luke gives us of the Son of man; His coming to His own country to begin His ministry and to the city where He had been brought up; His claiming in humble dependence the direction of the Holy Spirit as He gives His message; His modest recognition of the Holy Scriptures as the authority and foundation of His address, and then the character of this message with its infinite tenderness and grace and its broad and sweeping appeal to humanity with all its needs: all this coupled with His rejection by His own people gives to the incident of our text a peculiar propriety as the opening chapter of Luke's account of that wondrous ministry that was to be so broad in its scope and so gracious in its mercy and love. We might well inscribe over the scene the touching words of another evangelist, "He came unto His own and His own received Him not."

HE BEGAN AT NAZARETH.

Let us note the fact that He began at Nazareth, His own city. The evangelists, Matthew and Mark, describe a visit by our Lord to Nazareth much later in His ministry. We find the account in the sixth chapter of Mark and the thirteenth chapter of Matthew. Most of the harmonists of the Gospel identify that visit with the one recorded by Luke in our text. But it is contrary to Luke's custom to insert incidents out of their chronological order. He usually follows the law of sequence more exactly than any of the evangelists, and it would not be

like him to strain a point in this record
even for the sake of introducing this striking scene as a frontispiece in his Gospel.
Further, when we look at the facts related
in Matthew and Mark, we find them quite
different from the incident in Luke. They
tell us that the Lord performed several miracles of a minor character at this time and
while "He could do no great miracle because
of their unbelief," yet "He laid His hands on
a few sick folk and they recovered."

The accounts of these evangelists also
show that the disciples were with Him.
Luke's narrative makes no mention of any
disciples and it seems quite certain that if
they had been there, they would have inter-
posed in some way to protect Him from the
violence of the mob who tried to hurl Him
from the brow of the hill on which the city
was built. We are therefore justified, we
believe, in regarding this as an earlier visit
to Nazareth quite near the beginning of His
ministry and probably just after His visit
to Cana and the brief tarry in Galilee that
followed, just before His journey to Jerusalem. Probably He left Capernaum for Nazareth, taking His mother with Him and leav-

ing her there while He journeyed down to
Jerusalem.

How tender the interest connected with
His first message to His own people, and
how full of significance for us in connection
with our responsibility to be faithful witnesses to our own family circle and immediate friends. Have we been true to our testimony there? Perhaps, like Him, we shall
be rejected, but none the less should we be
faithful even if it must be as true of us as
of Him, "A prophet is not without honor
save in his own country and among his own
people."

IN THE SPIRIT.

Quite as remarkable is His dependence
upon the Holy Spirit in this, His first message. He does not come announcing His
own independent authority, but He takes
the place of one dependent upon the same
great Teacher to whom we all may look for
our endowment of power for service. There
is something very striking in the voluntary
dependence of the Lord Jesus upon the
power of the Holy Spirit in all His work and
teaching. Surely, if He did not venture upon
His ministry without the baptism of the

Spirit and did not take a step except in dependence upon Him, we are guilty of the
highest presumption should we attempt the
slightest ministry in our human strength.
How near it brings us to Him and Him to
us to find Him thus leaning upon the same
Arm that sustains us in all our service.

We cannot fail to note the effects of the
Spirit's baptism as manifested in our Lord.
"They all bare Him witness and wondered
at the gracious words which proceeded out
of His mouth." The Spirit-filled worker
will always have the same token, the unction
of the Holy Ghost as shown in every tone
and expression as a spirit of graciousness,
gentleness and power.

How may we expect to receive this power? Surely, by truly expecting it and claiming it by faith. There was no uncertain
sound in the confession of His faith. "The
Spirit of the Lord is upon Me," He could
say, and we too must claim this divine endowment as positively and confess it as
steadfastly. Are we thus working in the
power of the Spirit as well as walking in
fellowship with Him? They that look for
Him will not look in vain.

HIS DEPENDENCE UPON THE HOLY SCRIPTURES.

Not only did He look to the Spirit to guide and inspire Him, but He took the Bible as the foundation of His messages. Already He had proved its power in the hour of temptation and now He leans upon it as He goes forth to His work. Other teachers are accustomed, in founding a new religion, to bring out a new Bible; so we have the Bibles of Mohammedanism, Mormonism and similar delusions. Jesus Christ identified Himself with the Old Testament Scriptures, and on this occasion began His ministry by taking the prophetic scroll, from which they were accustomed to hear their morning lesson, and reading the very passage which was fulfilled that day in their ears in His own personal ministry.

We notice His familiarity with the prophetic Word. "When He had opened the scroll, He found the place where it was written." He knew where to find it. He was familiar with His Bible. Oh, that we, like Him, might be "workmen needing not to be ashamed, rightly dividing the Word of truth." The modern preacher soon exhausts his Bible and goes to the newspapers or the scientists for his sensational messages.

The wise preacher will always preach the Word. Not only so, but He also knew how to apply the Word to the occasion and the audience. "This day," He said, looking directly in the faces of His hearers, "is this Scripture fulfilled in your ears." His preaching was pointed, personal and intensely practical. So let ours be. Let us aim at men and women and let us strike hard at human consciences and hearts and let us expect immediate decisions and results.

HIS MESSAGE.

What a wonderful message it was! How fitting to the scope and purpose of Luke's Gospel! How different from the great sermon recorded by Matthew in the opening of his Gospel! That was suited for the Jew and the Gospel of the kingdom. It was all about "the kingdom of God and His righteousness." There is nothing of this in Luke, the Gospel of the Gentiles and the sinner. The keynote here is all grace, mercy and salvation.

THE GOSPEL OF THE JUBILEE.

The first note and the supreme note in it is joyfulness. It is a message of hope to a sorrowing, despairing world. It has been well called the Gospel of the Jubilee. Its undertone and its echo is gladness, victory, deliverance from all the evils that oppress humanity. It is the "sovereign balm for every wound." It is the remedy for the ills of humanity. Back of it stands the splendid figure of the Year of Jubilee. This is just the meaning of the closing clause to "proclaim the acceptable year of the Lord."

Every fifty years there came to ancient Israel a great festival that lasted a whole year long. All labor ceased and the earth abundantly supplied, the preceding year, enough for two. Nature rested, man rested and every home and synagogue and sanctuary and spot became the scene of festival and gladness. With its early dawn, the jubilee trumpets rang out upon every mountain top and summoned the people to a year of rejoicing, and, as the year wore on, you might have seen many a family moving back to the vine-clad cottage which they had been compelled to lose years before for some mortgage debt. You might have seen sons and daughters traveling home and welcomed by rejoicing fathers and mothers

as they came back from the slavery to which
they had been consigned as hostages for
some family debt. You might have seen
bonds and mortgages, promissory notes and
liens torn up or burned to ashes while every
debt was cancelled, every slave set free, every prison opened and every lost heritage
restored. All this Jesus Christ came to fulfil in a higher and grander sense by pro-
claiming an everlasting jubilee for all who
accept His grace. Surely, such a Gospel
is indeed humanity's greatest boon and the
announcement of such a message a fitting
and glorious inauguration of the Gospel of
the Son of man.

FORGIVENESS OF SINS.

Coming down to particulars, the first
great blessing of this jubilee is the cancell-
ing of our debt, the forgiveness of our sins
and the discharge for us of all our obligations to a broken law and an offended God.
Christ has come to set us free from the law,
not only from its curse and penalty, but
from its bondage as demanding our righteousness; giving us instead His better
righteousness and His indwelling and enabling, so that "the righteousness of the

law is fulfilled in us who walk not after the flesh, but after the Spirit." Have we entered into this glorious liberty? Have we taken Him for all our liabilities and responsibilities and are we proving that noble *Magna Charta* of the children of God, "Whom the Son makes free is free indeed"?

FREEDOM FROM SIN.

He brings freedom from the bondage of sin, "deliverance to the captives, liberty to them that are bruised." The sinner is helpless as well as guilty. He has gone upon the enemy's ground and has been taken captive. This does not lessen his accountability because he is responsible for having put himself in this condition, but he is none the less helpless. Sinful men are spoken of in the Scriptures as "taken captive by Satan at his will." "Wicked men are given over to a reprobate mind." Of course, they think they can do as they please, but they find when it comes to the test that they are "carnal sold under sin." One of the chains of sin is the force of habit. Another is an evil nature and a heart whose preference is for evil. We find an innate tendency to sin developed in the youngest children. From all this, Christ comes to set us free. "The law of the spirit of life in Christ Jesus hath made me free from the law of sin and death." The Holy Spirit puts within us a new heart, new thoughts, new desires and preferences and then He puts within us also new strength, His own power to enable us to obey these higher impulses.

> "He breaks the power of cancelled sin;
> He sets the prisoners free."

The bondage of sickness is also implied in this passage. "Them that are bruised" literally mean, "Them that are diseased." Sickness and death follow sin by the operation of the same great law. From sickness Christ sets us free by His healing power and from death He has delivered us by His resurrection, which is the pledge and guarantee of ours.

Oh, what a glorious announcement to a death-doomed and fallen race! What else can for a moment compare with the lofty claims and infinite and eternal possibilities of our great redemption?

OUR LOST INHERITANCE.

The jubilee gave back their lost inheritances. The home that had been forfeited for debt returned to its ancient owners and the inalienable possessions of the family were restored. Christ has come to give us back all which we, through sin, have lost; lost years, lost opportunities, lost powers, lost hopes, a lost heaven and our lost loved ones. The curse of sin is more than cancelled, and in Him we boast "more blessings than our father lost."

THE GRACE OF GOD.

The one underlying thought in all this glorious proclamation is grace. It is the revealing of the heart of God. It is a proclamation of infinite help to a helpless, hopeless world. "The acceptable year of the Lord" just means the day of grace, the offer of mercy, the opportunity of salvation for all who will receive and believe. It finds its parallel in that beautiful expression of the apostle in the Second Epistle to the Corinthians, "Behold, now is the accepted time; behold, now is the day of salvation." Literally, it means, "Now is the time of loving welcome; now is the day of salvation."

The most noticeable thing about this paragraph is that the Lord stopped in the mid-

dle of a sentence and omitted the last clause
of the quotation from Isaiah. That clause
is "The day of vengeance of our God." He
did not read this because the time for that
had not yet come. The day of grace is a
great parenthesis, but some time soon that
parenthesis will end and the prophecy will
be finished, and on a slumbering world will
burst "The day of vengeance of our God."
Oh, that we might catch the spirit of this
glorious evangel and go forth to ring it out
from all the mountain tops of earth until the
glad jubilee of the world will have fully
come with the coming of the King Himself
in His millennial glory!

The illustrations which our Lord adds in
His sermon at Nazareth are most significant. They are drawn from Hebrew history
and they both anticipate the dispensation of
the Gospel for the Gentiles. "Verily I say
unto you, many widows were in Israel in
the days of Elias, but to none of them was
Elias sent save unto Sarepta, a city of Si-
don, unto a woman that was a widow. And
many lepers were in Israel in the time of
Eliseus the prophet and none of them was
cleansed, saving Naaman, the Syrian."

How strange the citation of these two

cases showing the overflow of God's mercy
even in their own history as a nation to two
Gentiles. The widow of Sarepta was a poor
Gentile, Naaman the Syrian was a Gentile
too, and yet these are the only instances of
divine mercy which the Saviour mentions in
His argument to show how the nation has in
the past rejected God, and He has reached
men and women beyond the pale of Israel
altogether. So once more they are to reject their Messiah and the Gentiles are to
come in and inherit their privileges. It was
a foreshadowing of the very reception that
He was Himself to get that morning, for
no sooner had these words fallen from His
lips than the whole congregation fell upon
Him in angry violence, and, dragging Him
to the city, tried to hurl Him from the cliff
on which Nazareth was built, and He was
only saved by a divine miracle which suddenly took Him. we are not told how, from
their midst, and enabled Him to escape their
blind fury.

So Luke gives us this early intimation of
the rejection of the Messiah by His own people and the coming of the Gentiles instead.
How solemn and full of instruction the fact
that although clothed with the power of the

Holy Ghost, the Master's first message to
His own people at Nazareth seemed utterly
to fail. Let us not be surprised if sometimes our messages too appear to fall upon
dull or unbelieving ears. Sometimes we
shall be "a savor of life unto life," sometimes of "death unto death." Let us be willing to follow the Master everywhere even
when it means rejection for us too.

> "I'll share the cross of Jesus,
>   Its crucifixion bear;
> All hail reproach and sorrow
>   If Jesus leads me there."

Beloved, have we followed the Master in
the baptism of the Spirit? Have we entered
into the spirit of the glorious Gospel of the
Jubilee, and are we sounding out its message and sending forth the trumpets of salvation to herald on earth's mountain tops
the glorious message?

> "Go and tell them, go and tell them,
>   Jesus died for sinful men;
> Go and tell them, go and tell them,
>   He is coming back again."

Chapter VI.
THE SON OF MAN AND THE SINNER.

"The Son of man is come to seek and to save that which was lost" (Luke xix. 10).

"This Man receiveth sinners and eateth with them" (Luke xv. 2).

IN nothing is it true that God's thoughts and ways are as high as heaven above the earth as in His dealing with sin and sinners. Human nature goes either to the extreme of undue palliation or undue severity, either embraces or consumes the transgressor. Divine grace, while condemning sin with a holy severity unapproached by the severest human standards, at the same time meets the sinner with a tender grace and an almighty help and love of which this beautiful gospel affords a series of illustrations unequaled in any of the books of the New Testament. In this respect, Luke is indeed the gospel of the Son of man and of Him might be written over almost every chapter, "The Son of man is come to seek and to save that which was lost."

In the present chapter we shall present five pictures of Christ's grace in relation to sinners, most of them peculiar to Luke.

THE CALLING OF LEVI.

(Luke v. 27.)

While this incident is not peculiar to the Gospel of Luke, yet it forms the introduction to a number of incidents that are not related by any other evangelist and it gives us the keynote of the whole. Here we see especially the unconventional character of our Lord and the simple and informal way in which He came into contact with sinful men. He sat down in the home of Levi with the company of publicans and sinners in the most unaffected and natural way, and by tact and sympathy He won His way to the hearts of men rather than by stately messages and formal addresses. If we would be soul winners like Him, we must learn to be "all things to all men if by any means we may save some."

But the special lesson of this incident is the beautiful tact which Christ used to save men as links through which He was able to reach other men. Levi represented the class from which he came, and through him the Saviour was able to come in contact with a great multitude who would have naturally stood off from Him had He met them as a

Jewish rabbi; but as the friend of Levi they gladly received Him and doubtless others also "believed on Him and followed Him."

Have we used our past and the influence which even a sinful life may have caused over our fellow men to bring them to the Christ who has redeemed us from a life of sin?

THE SINFUL WOMAN IN THE HOUSE OF SIMON.

(Luke vii. 36-50.)

In looking at this touching example of our Saviour's love, it will help us to enter into the spirit of it if we recall the probable prelude to the story of Luke. This will be found in the closing verses of the eleventh chapter of the Gospel of Matthew. The beautiful words of invitation with which that paragraph closes, "Come unto Me all ye that labor and are heavy laden, and I will give you rest," would seem to have been spoken in immediate connection with this incident. Probably they form the close of an address which the Master had just been giving in some public place to the assembled crowd, and among those who heard it were both Simon and this sinful woman. On him

it had made a profound impression and with
evident sincerity he had invited the Lord to
come to his home and accept his hospitality. The evangelist tells us that he "desired Him to eat with him." This word
"desired" carries with it the idea of earnest
and perhaps repeated importunity. He was
evidently cordial and sincere in his invitation. The Master's own words in the parable that followed in the house of Simon
leaves no doubt that notwithstanding all
that was wrong in his spirit, he had been
forgiven. He was certainly one of the two
debtors referred to in the parable and Christ
says the Lord "frankly forgave them both."
We are not, therefore, to think of him as a
supercilious and scornful adversary, but as
an honest friend gradually emerging from
the prejudices of the Phariseeism in which
he had been so long schooled. The Lord ap-
preciates his spirit and in the scene which
follows is endeavoring to help him quite as
much as the sinful woman.

AN ORIENTAL SCENE.

The scene in the house of Simon is a striking one. Reclining at the table in a large
court, with their feet extending back from

the table on the Oriental divans, the guests
were assembled at meat; while around the
walls of the large chamber or court a mot-
ley crowd sometimes gathered, freely passing through the open doors according to the
simple etiquette of an Eastern home. There
was, therefore, no reason why this poor
woman of the town should not also slip in
with the crowd and take her place behind
the seated guests. The language of the
narrative implies that all this had been carefully planned by her. She had known that
Christ was to be there and she had chosen
the time to express her love and gratitude.
She had heard Him utter those gracious
words of invitation already quoted. Perhaps He had looked into her face and made
her know that her sins were forgiven. Certainly she had taken this by faith herself,
for the Lord clearly implies that her great
love was the result of a sense of great forgiveness.

The language of the narrative implies that
the gift she brought had been hers before.
Probably it was the wages of her sin, and
surely if ever gift was "tainted" this was.
But the Lord can accept the gifts of the vil-
est if they are accompanied by the tears that

show that the heart and hands that bring
them have been cleansed. She had evidently
meant to be calm and proper in her thank
offering, but before she knew it a storm of
feeling had swept all barriers away, and
she found her tears would not stay back as
she had bid them, but fell in torrents of pas-
sionate love and contrition at His feet.
Luke says, "She began to wet His feet with
her tears." That implies that she stopped
her weeping just as quickly as she could
compose herself, but already those tears
covered His holy feet and made it difficult
for her to anoint them as she had planned.
The tears were not in the program and so it
became necessary to wipe them away. Im-
pulsively she loosed her tresses and with
her hair she wiped away the tear stains from
His feet, and then she took the costly spike-
nard, and with many a caress of love she
anointed His blessed feet until the house
was filled with the odor of the oil.

THE TEMPTATION OF SIMON.

It had all been so sudden that the company of guests were held spellbound, and
Simon himself was the most impressed of
them all. Well he knew her character, and

expected his guests with becoming dignity
to check or rebuke this sudden interrup-
tion. What must have been his amazement
when he turned and saw the Saviour Himself evidently accepting with complacency
and approval this extraordinary demonstra-
tion. Immediately the confidence that had
started in his own heart began to be rudely
checked. Must he not be mistaken? Can
this man be a true prophet and not really
know the character of the woman who was
touching Him; or, if He knows, can He be
a good man to allow her to take such liber-
ties? Jesus understood his thought, and
quickly answered it. We do not need to
speak out for the Lord to know what is
passing in our hearts. Very striking are
the two expressions, "the Pharisee spake
within himself," and "Jesus answering, said
unto him." No word had come out from
those cold and haughty lips, but he had
spoken all the same, and Christ had heard
it. It would not do to let the temptation
be unmet. Simon must understand, and the
woman, too. And so that matchless parable
follows in which the guilt of both is pictured
in such discriminating and heart-searching
words, and then the grace of God to both is

6

pictured in the matchless language of the parable, and the gentle yet unmistakable reproof is suggested to the proud heart of the Pharisee, while to the sinful woman He addresses the reassuring words, her sins, which are ·many, are forgiven, "Thy faith hath saved thee, go in peace."

LESSONS.

For us the lesson is plain and full of the gospel of the grace of God.

1. We are all debtors.

2. There is a great difference in our debts. God does not condone gross sin, but characterizes it at its true estimation. Yes, her sins are many. There is no attempt to whitewash her life. It is all frankly conceded. She is a greater sinner than Simon, but

3. Both are equally bankrupt. They have nothing to pay. Simon can not meet his debt any more than the woman.

4. The free grace of God frankly forgives them both.

5. Love is not the crown of forgiveness, but the proof of it. She is much forgiven, therefore she loves much. Put in the word

"therefore," instead of "for," and you get the Gospel truth unmixed with error.

6. It was her faith that saved her, not her love; but her faith worked by love and melted her heart with tender gratitude for her forgiveness.

7. Forgiveness brings us into peace. "Come into peace," is the literal translation of the message of her Saviour; a land of rest, a new world of infinite and everlasting joy and doubtless in the coming days she was found with loving heart and willing hands among those that ministered to the Lord. This is the gospel of the grace of God. This is the attitude of Jesus Christ toward sinful men and women.

A SINFUL MAN.

Now it is not a sinful woman, but a sinful man, that meets us, and it is a new type of sin altogether. Perhaps before the world it may seem much more respectable. Here is no degrading lust, no repulsive debauchery and open vice, and yet here is perhaps the hardest and most hopeless of all the forms of human sin: the love of money. But there is a key even to the heart of Zaccheus. That key is the love and grace of the Lord Jesus Christ. The Master did not wait until Zaccheus had sought Him, for Christ Himself was seeking this poor lost sinner. How sublime the grace that offers itself to the sinner unsought and unconditionally! "Zaccheus, make haste and come down, for to-day I must abide at thy house." So the Master gave Himself unreservedly, unconditionally to this hard and sinful man, and what was the result? Listen: Zaccheus stood and cried, "Lord, the half of my goods I give to the poor, and if I have taken anything from any man by false accusation, I restore him fourfold." That was the repentance that comes from one touch of divine grace. So the sunrise melts away the fogs of night. So the summer melts away the frosts of winter. So the Gulf Stream embraces in its mighty arms the icebergs of the Pole and lo, they fall into that warm and fertilizing stream that turns the shores of Western Europe into summer lands. And so the grace of God transforms the hardest heart.

But above all other impressions that we gather from this matchless picture, there is none more touching than what Robertson of Brighton has so happily called "Christ's estimate of sin."

Speaking of Zaccheus, He does not seem to think of his hardness, his meanness, his selfishness, but only of his danger. In the thought of Christ, it was enough that he was lost and He had come to seek and save him. So Christ is looking at every sinner still with a deep concern that is only too glad to forgive the past if only He may save for the present and future. Oh, that we may have that love for sinful men, for perishing men!

CHRIST WEEPING OVER JERUSALEM.

(Luke xix. 41-44.)

The one touching yet terrific truth that stands out above all others from this dramatic picture is that marvelous love that can still pity when it is too late to save. As Christ looked down upon that doomed city lying at His feet, He knew that the day of grace was already past, but none the less did He cry, "If thou hadst known, even thou, at least in this thy day, the things which belong unto thy peace, but now they are hid from thine eyes." Blessed Heart of infinite

and everlasting love, it is sweet to know
that even when we will not let Thee save us,
we can not keep Thee from loving us. Surely, this should be enough to touch every
sinner's heart and drive him to the feet of
Jesus.

There is a day of grace, and it passes even
long before the thunders of judgment roll
and the lightnings of doom burst from the
angry clouds. All may be calm, certain and
free from alarm, and yet the soul be lost and
Christ only have for you the mercy of His
tears.

THE DYING THIEF.

(Luke xxiii. 39-43.)

This is not peculiar to Luke in one sense,
for two of the other evangelists refer to it,
but Luke only gives the details. They seem
to have just mentioned it, and then remembered that it was best suited for the gospel
of the Son of man and left it for Luke to tell
the story in detail.

It is inexpressibly touching that Luke
should make it the last scene in the Saviour's life, for as he finishes his narrative we
hear Him gently say, "Father, into Thy
hands I commit My Spirit," and with that

first ransomed sinner in His arms Jesus has entered Paradise. His last act on earth was to save a brutal murderer; His first in heaven was to present him washed and glorified before His Father's throne. Surely, this was a fitting picture for the Gospel of the Son of man.

What is the supreme message of this scene in connection with our subject? Surely it is this: that the destiny of the sinner depends upon his attitude toward the cross of Jesus Christ. There were two sinners there that day, "on either side one and Jesus in the midst," and while one went with the Redeemer into Paradise, the other passed with curses upon his wicked lips from Calvary to perdition, and the only reason was that the one accepted Jesus as his Saviour and the other refused Him. What a message of warning as well as encouragement! How awful to think that we may find the way to hell from the very side of the crucified Redeemer, as well as the way to heaven in the last moment of life from the depths of a life of wickedness by simple faith in the Son of man.

Dear reader, on which side of that cross are you?

Chapter VII.

THE SON OF MAN AND THE HOME.

"Now it came to pass, as they went, that He entered into a certain village and a certain woman named Martha received Him into her house. And she had a sister called Mary, which also sat at Jesus' feet and heard His Word. But Martha was cumbered about much serving and came to Him and said, Lord, dost Thou not care that my sister hath left me to serve alone? Bid her therefore that she help me. And Jesus answered and said unto her, Martha, Martha, thou art careful and troubled about many things. But one thing is needful and Mary hath chosen that good part which shall not be taken away from her" (Luke x. 38-42).

WE have here another woman at the feet of Jesus, but how different from the former scene. This one is listening, learning, loving and leaving her sweet lesson of higher service for all the ages.

THE SON OF MAN AND THE HOME.

How sacred is the home circle and the hearth stone. There we begin our life. There usually we close it. And with it the sweetest joys and the most sacred memories of life are associated. Luke and John give us a picture of the Son of man in the home at Bethany. From the crowded city He loved to retire at night to the quiet surroundings and loving society of the household of Bethany, and we love still to think of Him as interested in our homes and the unseen Guest in every family circle. He began His public ministry at the marriage of Cana in Galilee and every word and act of His life gave a higher sanction to the sacredness of family life.

Has Christ His true place in our homes? Do we minister to Him at the family altar, and do we sit, like Mary, at His feet and give Him the greater joy of ministering unto us?

This incident has given us two companion pictures hung up in the galleries of time, and revealing to us two types of Christian life intensely real and strangely different.

THE SPIRIT OF MARTHA.

1. She was a friend of Christ. With all her faults and shortcomings, she loved her Master well, and it is distinctly stated, "Now Jesus loved Martha and her sister and Lazarus." Let us never forget, amid all our faults and the faults of our friends, that Christ loves our imperfect lives and

will not leave us until He has done His very best for every one of us.

2. The motive of her service on this occasion was love. She was mistaken in her method. She was excessive in her preparations and attentions, but her heart was true. She spoiled her work, but through all its defects, the Master saw that true and tender heart and loved her none the less. How full of mistakes our service often is. How comforting to know that we have a Master and a Judge who loves to detach the imperfections from our gifts of devotion, and accept them through His own merits as if they were blameless.

3. Martha represents the practical Christian. Her love found expression through her hands, her eyes, her busy brain. There is a type of womanly character which a New England writer has called "faculty" which is a little in danger of detracting from the feminine qualities of many good women. They are tempted to elbow aside their quieter sisters and to fall either into masculine boldness or feminine fussiness. You practical people need the balance wheel which Mary had, of a heart that has learned to sit

at the feet of Jesus as well as run around and serve.

4. Martha was too particular about mere external things. Her housekeeping and her hospitality were overdone. This is the fault of many good women to-day. They are in bondage to their homes, and they are allowing style, equipage and entertainment to hinder the development of higher qualities and the fulfilment of higher ministries.

5. Martha was restless. "Thou art careful and troubled," might be translated, "Thou art fussing and fretting." Anxious care and mental agitation are always wrong. We should never be driven by our work. We should never lose our poise or peace. "Be anxious about nothing." "Let the peace of God rule in your hearts."

6. Worse than all this was Martha's ill temper. This is a great fault in all, but a fatal blemish in a woman. There are two jewels she should always wear: namely, quietness and sweetness. No matter how beautiful or brilliant you may be, ill temper will deface your beauty and neutralize your usefulness.

7. Rudeness and discourtesy also characterized Martha's conduct. She publicly ex-

posed her irritation against her sister and
she even went so far as to blame the Lord
Himself for allowing her to act as she had
done. We think our irritation is all against
people and things, but really it is against
God.   When Israel murmured against
Moses, God took it all to Himself. Martha
was not the first that found fault with the
Lord because He did not straighten out the
disagreeable people. When we come with
such requests to Christ, we shall usually
find that He will turn the tables upon us and
proceed to straighten us out. The trouble
is nearer home. "Love doth not behave itself unseemly." A Christian woman should
always be a lady. A Christian man should
always be a gentleman. If you have fault to
find with your brother, go to him alone and
tell him. "Showing all gentleness toward all
men."

8. Another of Martha's troubles was the
many things that concerned her. Her heart
was divided. Her mind was distracted. She
had too many aims in life. She needed sin-
gleness of purpose. This is the trouble with
us all. If we are seeking first the kingdom
of God and His righteousness, we shall be,

less worried about other things and we shall leave Him to add them to us.

9. Martha's worst fault was that she failed to understand her Lord. She thought that He wanted her to do something for Him, when in reality He was just wanting to do something for her.

How Christ must be pained and disappointed with the people that are spending their lives in ecclesiastical millinery and religious ceremonies, serving tables and performing pageants of worship under the impression that this is acceptable service to Him. "To what purpose," He asks, "is the multitude of your sacrifices unto Me?" "If I were hungry, I would not tell thee, for the world is Mine and the fulness thereof. Will I eat the flesh of bulls or drink the blood of goats? Offer unto God thanksgiving. Pay thy vows unto the Most High and call upon Me in the day of trouble, and I will deliver thee and thou shalt glorify Me."

THE PICTURE OF MARY.

1. In the first place, Mary had not been neglectful of her practical duties. She had done her part in the kitchen, and at a certain point, thinking that enough was done,

she had left Martha and taken her place at
the feet of Jesus. This is implied in the
aorist tense, "She hath left me to serve
alone." She had been serving and simply
changed the form of her service. Mary
therefore was as practical as Martha, but she
did not carry it too far. In our spiritual
ministries we must be careful not to neglect
our human relationships and duties. Our
husbands and children should not suffer
while we are sitting at the feet of Jesus.
But the most spiritual people can be the
most practical. "Not slothful in business,
but fervent in spirit serving the Lord."

2. The secret of Mary's happier temper
was that she was not living for many things,
but for one thing. "One thing is needful,
and Mary hath chosen that good part."
Hers was an undivided heart. Hers was a
life that had sought the best things, and let
the world and its distractions go.

3. She had sought the best things. How
many people take the second best! There is
a fine play upon the words here in the expression, "That good part." The Romans,
at their splendid feasts, were accustomed to
have a choice morsel for the guest of honor.
This phrase literally means "the choice bit."

The Lord uses the very figure that appeals to Martha, taken from her own domestic department. She thought she knew what was the best, but Mary had the advantage of her and had chosen it and received it. With all his faults, this was the one distinguishing point between Jacob and Esau. There was very much about Jacob that was unattractive. He was selfish and contriving and full of cunning, but he knew the value of the blessing and the birthright. He appreciated the highest things and God loved him for it and gave him what he chose. So we shall get what we choose.

4. Mary had learned to receive rather than to try to give. She understood the meaning of grace and that the Lord had come, not to get our help, but to give us His help and blessing. This is the very height of grace as taught in the Word of God. Martha still was full of the spirit and of the law. She wanted to serve, to work, to do something. Mary had learned that Jesus had come to put an end to our doing and to give us in exchange His grace. Therefore to-day God draws a line between people at this very point. "They that receive abundance of grace and the gift of righteousness shall

reign in life by One"; while those who try
to work their way will find, like Israel of
old, "going about to establish their own
righteousness" they have not submitted unto
the righteousness of God.

5. It all comes to this: that Mary understood her Lord and Martha failed to understand Him. Mary comprehended the real
heart of Jesus and the object that had
brought Him from heaven, and Martha was
still under the old spirit of Judaism. A little later, when once again the Master sat
at that table in Bethany, Mary was the only
one of all that company that comprehended
the things that were pressing upon His heart
and the great purpose which had brought
Him to the world: to die for sinful men.
It was this that cheered the heart of Jesus:
that she understood Him, and when she
poured that precious ointment upon His feet
He declared with words of profound significance, "She hath come beforehand to anoint
My body for the burial." Mary understood
Him and, instead of waiting like the other
women to anoint Him after He was dead,
and finding, as they did, that He had already
arisen and the opportunity was gone, Mary
came beforehand and sent Him forth to His

great Priesthood with an intelligent faith
and devoted love that took away much of
the sharpness of that bitter cross.

Beloved, do we understand the Saviour?
Do we enter into His thought? Do we give
Him our sympathy, our fellowship, our
deepest love? Mary represents through all
the ages the spiritual life in contrast with
the practical and yet as the true inspiration
of all practical holiness. We must first come
to Him and learn to sit at His feet, hear His
word and receive His grace before we can
give Him back anything in return that will
be worthy of His receiving. God is not
blaming us because we do not give more,
but because we do not take more. The keynote of redemption is grace. It is through
grace alone that we can receive the first
touches of the new life, but it is equally
through grace that we must serve Him all
the way. "All things come of Thee and of
Thine own have we given Thee."

OUR CHOICE.

There is a very practical and helpful word
in this incident that will answer for most
of us the question: How can we have the
best things that God has for us? The an-

7

swer is found in that little word "chosen."
"Mary hath chosen." It was not with Mary
a matter of temperament, making her con-
templative rather than practical. It was a
matter of will. She had chosen deliberately,
intelligently, the best that God had for her.
A fine old German saint was once asked
why it was that we did not have more holiness, and his answer was, "We have all the
holiness we want. God will sanctify you,
and does sanctify every one of us just as
much as we wish and choose." This is a
heart-searching truth. God gives us what
we want. If you want a little of His grace,
you may get it. If you want to be half-
hearted, you may. But if you want to be
wholly His and have all His fulness, His
great heart is just longing to find room and
vent for His love, and "He will open unto
you the windows of heaven and pour out a
blessing until there shall not be room to
receive it."

CHAPTER VIII.

THE SON OF MAN AND THE FIRST DISCIPLES.

"Fear not, from henceforth thou shalt catch men" (Luke v. 10).

NOTHING is more in keeping with the perfect humanity of the Lord Jesus Christ than the fact that He committed His work so fully to the hands of His disciples. His own personal ministry did not result in the conversion of as many people apparently as were added to the church in a single day under the preaching of His servant Peter. Like Solomon, who committed his work to the hands of David and rejoiced to see it prosper in his hands, so the blessed Master loves to work through His disciples. He, the true Vine, does not bear the fruit Himself, but rather gives it to the little branches and the youngest sprouts to be loaded with the precious clusters while the Vine sustains them with its life.

While the Lord Jesus had already called His disciples at various times to follow Him, it would seem that they had not yet abandoned their ordinary vocations and devoted themselves exclusively to His service.

On His visit to Nazareth shortly before
this, He was unaccompanied by His disciples and on this occasion we find them still
upon the shores of the Lake of Galilee attending to their ordinary business as fisher-
men. The call that comes to them at this
time leads to their final separation from all
other conflicting interests, and the devotion
of their lives exclusively to the service of
the Lord. His call to Simon and his fellow
disciples reaches a wider company and
teaches us many useful lessons about our
service for the Lord.

GOD CALLS US THROUGH OUR SECULAR OCCUPA-
TION.

He found Saul seeking his father's asses.
He found Samuel attending to his duties in
the house of Eli. He found Moses shep-
herding the flocks of Jethro. He found
David occupied with his sheep at Bethlehem.
He found the shepherds of the advent morn-
ing engaged in their duties and vocations.
He found Elisha ploughing his fields at
Abel-Meholah. And He found Simon at his
fishing nets in Bethsaida.

So He will meet us also at our daily tasks
and enable us to turn them to higher ac-

count. We need not give up our callings to serve the Lord unless He clearly shows us that He would have us to do so, but serve Him in our secular duties with a consecrated spirit, and when He calls us to higher service, we shall find the lessons we learned in the school of life will be fraught with holy power for the ministries of heaven.

HE CAME TO THEM WHEN THEY HAD FAILED IN THEIR EARTHLY CALLING.

They had toiled all night and caught nothing, and then it was that He met them with the miraculous draught of fishes and said, "Fear not, from henceforth thou shalt catch men." So God comes to us through our earthly trials and opens to us a vision of higher work. But for Joseph's trials, he would never have been able to save his father's house and feed the famine of the whole world. Had not poverty and widowhood come upon Naomi in the land of Moab, the beautiful story of Ruth would have been unwritten and she had had no part in the glorious history of Israel and the Messiah. It was when the widow of Zarephath had only a single handful of meal and a single drop of oil left that the higher call came to her to

feed the prophet of the Lord and to receive
the most glorious manifestation of Divine
power in the whole history of the Old Testament. It is said that Adam Clark failed
completely as a clerk in a commercial house
before he found his higher ministry to teach
the children of God and the churches of later
centuries.

There is some lesson in your business failure. There is some blessing hidden behind
the cloud if you will only watch for the coming of the Son of man and follow as He leads.

CHRIST ASKS SERVICE FROM SIMON.

"He entered into Simon's ship and prayed
him that he would thrust out a little from
the land," and then turning the fishing boat
into a pulpit, He began to preach to the people from the stern of the little ship.

So He came to the woman of Samaria and
asked her for a drink of water and then He
gave her the living water and the glorious
ministry of telling the story of Christ to her
own wondering people. So again He came
to Zaccheus and asked that He might stay
at his house for entertainment, but He
brought with Him a whole heaven of higher
blessing.

So He calls upon us for some little ministry; some gift to help a poor and suffering life; some act of self-denial for His service, and the joy it brings to us is so great that we never can rest again till we have entered upon His service and given Him all our life. He comes to us with deepest condescension. He prayed Simon for the use of his little ship that day. He is praying us to give to Him our hearts and standing, as He pleads, "Behold, I stand at the door and knock; if any man will hear My voice I will come into him and sup with him and he with Me."

Shall we listen to His tender appeal and let Him lead us up to the noblest service and the most glorious and lasting blessing?

THE VALUE OF HARD PLACES.

Had Daniel remained the petted courtier in the palace at Jerusalem, he never could have been God's chosen instrument to bring Nebuchadnezzar to the feet of Jehovah and glorify God before the heathen world. It was the ordeal of the fiery furnace and the lions' den that brought out the grandeur of his faith and the power of his God.

The life of Paul was one continuous succession of hardships so that he could say he was made "a spectacle unto angels and men" of the power of God to sustain a suffering child. Each new trial enabled him to say, "The things that have happened unto me have turned out unto the furtherance of the Gospel."

And so God has to push us out into some new place of difficulty in order to develop our faith and show us what He can do for us and through us. You will never know how God can use you until you venture upon Him and attempt more than you are equal to in your own strength and resources. The first time you attempted to give a simple testimony for Christ, you hesitated and feared the very sound of your own voice; but when you launched out and ventured upon Him, you found your voice and your work, and ever afterwards you had liberty and power in witnessing for the Master. The late Mrs. Booth was literally pushed into her public work by her husband suddenly committing to her one day a public service for which she had no experience or training whatever, and from which she shrank back with extreme sensitiveness and dread. But finding herself alone and compelled to say something, she opened her lips in dependence upon God, and to her own amazement and the delight of her hearers, she found that God had given her an unction of which she had never dreamed, and which, but for that venture, would have been unused and lost. This is why our fellow workers upon the heathen field grow so fast in their spiritual life. Their difficulties mold them. Their hard places challenge for them the richer gifts and graces of the Spirit and as they "launch out into the deep" they find the Master is with them and that great shoals of fishes are to be gathered in.

Dear reader, wherefore tarry in your diffidence and false humility and fail to attempt some bold service for the Master. Arise in your strength and giving up both your strength and weakness to Him, go forth to "attempt great things for God and expect great things from God."

GOD'S PROVIDENCE.

Christ manifested Himself in the miraculous draught of fishes to Simon and his brethren, and astonished and inspired them by the vision of His power.

So God meets us in some hard place in life by the angels of His providence, and the interposition of His power until we too are

filled with awe and praise at some marvelous deliverance, and henceforth we never
can be the same again. Such places in our
life are like "the land of Jordan and the hill
Mizar," to which David looked back as the
sunlit peaks of life's mountains; the places
where God meets us and the heavens are
opened in the revelation of His love and
power. This forever makes life divine and
God intensely real. God is waiting to meet
us along life's pathway with just such memo-
rials and fills our hearts with confidence
in His all-sufficiency and power; and if He
has so met us let us "not be disobedient to
the heavenly vision," but remember that our
life is a trust, and that God has simply
shown us what He is able to do for us a
thousand times if we will but step out upon
His Word and venture upon His almighty
help.

GOD'S WORD.

It was the word of the Master that called
Simon to higher service. "Nevertheless at
Thy word will I let down the net." It is a
crisis hour in our life when first the Word of
God becomes real to us. Up to that time it
was just a book, but now it becomes a mes-

sage. It was that Word that came to Moses,
to Samuel, to Elisha, to Paul, and transformed their lives. If we will listen, we will
hear it speaking with divine authority to
our conscience and heart and saying, "Follow Me." When God speaks to us and
sends us forth at His command, then no danger can appal us and no difficulty can dis
courage us. Oh, what a condescension that
the Mighty One should turn aside and call
us, insignificant children of the dust, to be
His fellow workers and partners of His very
throne. God grant that even as you read
these lines, some heart may discern that
voice and answer, "Rabboni."

THE REVELATION OF SELF.

This miracle brought to Simon Peter not
only the revelation of Christ, but a revelation of himself. "Depart from me," he cried,
"for I am a sinful man, O Lord." The vision of God always disgusts us with ourselves. There need be no discouragement in
this deep consciousness of our unworthiness.
It will but make larger room for God Himself and bring us into closer sympathy with
weak and sinful men. God show us Himself
and ourselves.

A CALL TO A DEEPER LIFE.

The call to Peter may be translated as a call to each of us to come into a deeper Christian life. Such an experience is the best qualification of Christian service. It is what we are more than what we say or do that God uses to impress other lives.

Have we gone down into the depths of self-surrender and have we ventured out into the ocean of His boundless grace? "Launch out into the deep and let down your nets for a draught."

SEPARATION.

The Master's message to Simon and his brethren led them to an entire separation to Him and His service. "They left all and followed Him"; their nets, their fathers, their old ties, interests and aims. Henceforth there was but one thing to live and labor for: the Master's work and will. Are we thus separated unto His service? Even if we still are led to continue in our secular callings, have we the separated spirit and the single aim?

THE PLACE OF SERVICE.

The end and purpose of all God's dealings

with us is service. "I will make you fishers of men." The word "men" is very emphatic here in the original. There is a suggestion that many of us are fishing for very poor game. Are we catching men? Oh, the value of a single soul! Think of one such life as Ramabai saved from the wreckage of India and the thousands of precious lives that she has brought to her King. What if God should give you one such soul in heathen lands? Oh, the glorious fruition which some day will meet us from lives of consecrated service! This is but the apprenticeship of our immortal life. There we shall enter upon unknown glories and we shall find that they will simply be the outcome of our life below.

In a recent poem Kipling has touched with a master hand, although with a very unconventional touch, the vision of the future. His striking picture is worth repeating:

"When Earth's last picture is painted,
    And the tubes are twisted and dried,
When the oldest color has faded,
    And the youngest critic has died—
We shall rest; and faith, we shall need it,
    Lie down for an æon or two,
Till the Master of all good workmen
    Shall set us to work, anew.

"And they who are good shall be happy,
  And sit in a golden chair,
And splash at a ten-league canvas
  With brushes of comet's hair.
They shall have real saints to draw from,
  Magdalene, Peter and Paul;
And work for an age at a sitting,
  And never get tired at all.

"And only the Master shall praise us,
  And only the Master shall blame,
And no one shall work for money,
  And no one shall work for fame.
But each for the joy of working,
  And each, in his separate star,
Shall paint the thing as he sees it,
  For the God of things as they are."

God has provided some better thing even
than this. "He that reapeth receiveth wages
and gathereth fruit unto life eternal: that
both he that soweth and he that reapeth may
rejoice together."

CHAPTER IX.

THE PARABLES OF DIVINE MERCY.

"I came not to call the righteous, but sinners, to repentance" (Luke v. 32).

THERE are fourteen parables peculiar to the Gospel of Luke, and singularly appropriate to his picture of the Son of man. They naturally divide themselves into two series, namely: parables of divine mercy, and parables of human destiny. The first seven are parables of divine mercy. The three parables of the fifteenth chapter of Luke form a trinity in unity. The other four also form a cluster by themselves and present a striking and complete view of the mercy of God. The first, the Good Samaritan, illustrates God's mercy to the fallen; the next, the Friend at Midnight, help in time of need; the third, the Great Supper, mercy for the suffering and outcast, and the fourth, the Pharisee and Publican, pardon for the penitent, and rejection for the self-righteous.

THE GOOD SAMARITAN, OR, MERCY FOR THE FALLEN.

(Luke x. 25-27.)

While in its first application this beautiful parable is of course designed to exemplify the duties of humanity and kindness to our neighbor, in answer to the Lord's question, "Who is my neighbor?" and in illustration of the Lord's teaching about love; yet deeper than all this it unfolds the glorious picture of the Lord Jesus Himself as the Friend and Deliverer of ruined and helpless sinners. The unhappy traveler, attacked, robbed, almost murdered on his way down from Jerusalem to Jericho, is the type of the sinner who on his downward path has fallen into the hands of Satan, and been stripped of his raiment, wounded in every part of his soul and body, and left, not only half dead, but spiritually dead in trespasses and sins.

THE PASSERSBY.

The priest and the Levite who pass him by in his misery, represent the failure of all human resources, and all human schemes of benevolence and reform, to reach and relieve

his distress. The first stands for Jewish sac-
erdotalism, and the cold and selfish priesthood of every age; and the other for hu-
manitarianism in all its forms and failures.
The lowly despised Samaritan is a good type
of the rejected Nazarene. "Say we not well
that thou art a Samaritan, and hast a devil?"
was the very germ of the treatment that the
Pharisees gave to Jesus; and He is willing
for a time to accept the obloquy, and to
glorify it by the love that puts to shame all
their pretensions. And so this good Samaritan does for the unfortunate traveler what
none of the others had thought of doing.
Although the man has no sort of a claim
upon him, and has perhaps also regarded
him as an enemy and an alien, yet the sight
of his distress is enough to call forth all his
love and strength for instant help and deliverance. First, he goes right to him, un-
deterred by fear of lurking enemies and a
similar fate himself. Next, he has compassion on him; his whole heart swells with
tenderness and pity, and all thought of selfishness is at once driven out by the one
overwhelming impulse of sympathy and
love. Then with his own hands, tenderly
bending over him, he binds up his hideous

8

wounds, pouring in oil and wine. And
when the poor victim is able to rise, he gently seats him on his own beast, conducts him
to the nearest inn, takes him to a chamber,
and watches tenderly by his side all the
night; and on the morrow he departs, pays
in advance for his expenses, and gives his
pledge to see that all else he may need shall
be honorably paid for when he comes again.

CHRIST, THE GOOD SAMARITAN.

What an exquisite picture of the love and
compassion of Christ. First, He pities us.
Then He comes to us even before we go to
Him. He heals the wounds of our sin; yes,
even of our body. He pours in the oil of
His Holy Spirit in comforting, quickening,
and healing love and power, and revives us
with the wine of His own love and joy. He
does not send us on our way alone, but carries us Himself, bearing us in His own arms,
or walking by our side. The inn in which
He shelters His rescued ones, is the blessed
Church of Christ. There He Himself takes
care of us, watching all through the night
of our trial; and when He seems to pass on
and withdraw His more manifest presence,
He still leaves ample provision for all our

need, and assures us that everything we can require is already paid for, and may be freely drawn from the resources of grace. And best of all, He adds the precious promise that He is coming again; and that every kindness rendered to His brethren, shall receive a hundredfold recompense.

THE FRIEND AT MIDNIGHT: OR HELP IN TIME OF NEED.

(Luke xi. 1-13.)

This beautiful parable leads us a step in advance of the other. There the sufferer is helpless and ready to die, and does not even ask or hope for deliverance. Mercy finds him in his misery, and brings to him unsought her gracious deliverance. This parable, however, represents the Divine mercy as given in response to the prayers of the needy. It is introduced by the lesson on prayer which the Lord Jesus gave to His disciples in response to their petition, "Lord, teach us to pray, as John also taught his disciples." First, He gives them a beautiful pattern prayer, the simplest and most universal liturgy of all Christendom. Then He illustrates the principle of prayer by this

beautiful parable, in which God is represented under the figure of a friend and a father;
and the case of distress is one of extreme
emergency. The need is not a personal,
but a relative one. The help is required for
a friend who has come at a late hour of the
night; and his host has kindly taken him in,
but has nothing to set before him. In this
situation, he appeals to his friend. But it
is an unseasonable, and almost an unreason-
able request. The time for visitors is long
past. The doors are all closed, and his children are with him in bed. The whole figure represents a case in which all probabili-
ty, even of Divine help, seems cut off, and
every door shut. It is at such a time as this
that the friend presumes upon the kindness
of his benefactor. It is a case where even
friendship probably would have been refused. But the parable teaches us that
where the claims of human kindness would
not have been strong enough, Divine mercy
breaks through every barrier, and meets the
cry of distress with instant and ample aid.
"I tell you though he will not rise and give
him because he is his friend, yet because of
his importunity, he will give him as many as
he needs." Dr. Walker, in his profound

book on the Holy Spirit, states that the word "importunity" here does not mean urgency on the part of the suppliant, but rather emergency in his situation—the extreme distress in which his benefactor saw he was, and on account of which his kind, compassionate heart rose above all difficulties, and immediately relieved him.

First, we have God in the two figures of Father and Friend.

Secondly, we see His willingness to help us, not only in season, but out of season; when the door of mercy even seems to be closed, and the time to help seems to have passed.

Thirdly, we see His consideration for the extremity of our circumstances, and the fact that the more difficult the case is, the more likely and willing He is to help.

Fourthly, we see the completeness and generosity of His provision; "as many as he needeth." The three loaves for which the friend asks, may well express the threefold fulness of the Gospel; salvation from past sins, and future judgment; sanctification from the power of evil; and temporal deliverance both from sickness, sorrow and all the other troubles and needs of life.

OUR NEED AND GOD'S RESOURCES.

And finally we find how much stronger
the claim we have upon His bounty and
help, not for our selfish needs, but for those
that we wish to relieve, either temporally or
spiritually, who have come to us in their distress, and we have nothing to set before
them. Even in our utmost helplessness and
need we may venture to undertake the most
difficult services for others; and then as we
go to Him, we shall find Him ready to meet
all our need. There is something beautiful
in the boldness of this man's faith, in taking
in the midnight wayfarer when he knew
that he had nothing to set before him. He
seemed to have such confidence in his friend,
that he ventured to the utmost length in the
exercise of his own hospitality. Surely we
may venture as far in undertaking the bur-
dens of Christ's work and the relief of His
suffering ones, in full assurance that even in
the most extreme case He will prove faithful
to us and place at our command His abun-
dant and unfailing resources. What an encouragement to us in the work of His kingdom; in every work before us; in charitable
relief for the orphan and the helpless; when
done in accordance with His wise and holy

will; and in all our spiritual work where we are conscious of our own insufficiency, and must constantly venture out in the confidence that He will supply as we go forward, the wisdom, and the power, the faith, and the love, the agencies, and the efficiency for all our service.

THE PARABLE OF THE GREAT SUPPER; OR, MERCY FOR THE SUFFERING AND OUTCAST.

(Luke xiv. 12-24.)

This parable represents the provisions of Divine mercy, under the figure of the feast long prepared, and now at last, complete. "All things are ready"—mercy to pardon, grace to purify, and power to keep. The invitations are sent out, and they are issued on a scale of almost boundless generosity. Three classes are successively invited.

THE WORLDLINGS.

First, the friends of the host, who here represent the ordinary hearers of the Gospel; perhaps we may say the worldly and nominal adherents of Christianity. They rejected the invitation. They did it very politely, as proud and worldly sinners still do.

The first class declined on account of pressing business engagements; perhaps connected with first starting in life, and beginning to acquire earthly possessions. This man has bought his piece of ground. He is just commencing to accumulate wealth, and is too busy to go to the feast. The second has bought five yoke of oxen. This represents an advanced stage of worldly success and occupation; he is now getting to be a very busy man. He is stocking his farm by the half score at a time, and rapidly growing rich. And so he for the present, puts off the kind invitation. The third has married a wife, and is still more peremptory in his refusal. He *cannot* come; and evidently he regards the religion of Jesus as incompatible with the thorough enjoyment of the pleasures of the world. Everything in its place. The bridal party, the honeymoon, the dance and revel are inconsistent in his view with the table of the Lord; and he allows the endearments, attachments, and pleasures of life to outweigh the claims of Christ, and the value of his soul.

The three forms of worldly obstruction which here stand in the way of the Gospel are worldly business, worldly wealth and worldly pleasure. With some, it is the eager desire to grow rich. With some, it is the increasing preoccupation of constant drive and absorbing business. With others, it is the love of pleasure and the influence of friends. From these various causes the great proportion of the invited guests still stay away from Christ. Indeed, the parable represents every one of them as refusing. It looks as though the whole body of nominal professors was ultimately going to reject the Gospel.

THE WORLD'S POOR.

Next comes a different class. The Master is not going to let His bounty be lost because these proud and contemptuous worldlings did not appreciate it. He is very angry with their contemptuous excuses. He does not look lightly on the sin of rejecting the great salvation. With calm and awful dignity He declares that none of these men shall taste of His bounty; takes every one at their word, and excuses them all. And now He sends out His servants into the streets and lanes of the city; not into the fine avenues, but into the narrow alleys where the poor are found in their wretchedness. Two classes especially, are described, the poor

and the sick. No doubt these are literally
meant, and the provision of the Gospel for
the temporal needs and physical ills of humanity is surely set forth in this picture. It
is, indeed, God's benison for the world's
poor. Most of its saved ones have come
from their ranks. Without it, life has little
for them. With it, it has not any grief to
harm them, and great is their reward in
heaven. It alleviates their physical condition. It is of infinite value even in improv-
ing the material condition of the poor, and
leading to prosperity and success in temporal things. And for the maimed, and the
halt, and the blind, it has not lost its ancient power of healing and uplifting them
from their temporal distresses. What a
mercy it would be for the poor if they could
but fully trust the Lord Jesus as their Heal-
er and physical Redeemer, as many of them
do, and find in Him the balm for every pain
and the remedy for every trial.

THE SINFUL.

Thirdly, there is another class. The Gospel is not satisfied when it has relieved the
physical ills and social miseries of men. And
so the servant comes back with the message,

"And yet there is room." The feast is not
exhausted with all the multitudes of suffering poor that have already sat down. The
tables still have room for myriads more; and
nothing must remain or go to waste, of all
this costly provision. So the messengers are
sent forth for the third time, and now they
go beyond the city walls to the highways
and hedges. It will at once occur to the
thoughtful reader that this is the place
where the lepers and outcasts herd together
in homeless misery, and unpitied exclusion.
These poor children of the wayside surely
stand for the outcast members of society; for
the lost and sinful who have passed even
beyond the pale of hope, and for whom there
seems to be no possibility of redemption,
or reformation; the degraded drunkard, the
dishonored daughter of shame and every
corruption, the criminal, the social pariahs
of life; yes, the Gospel has ample room and
almighty power for all these. But they are
not expected to appreciate it or embrace it
of their own accord. Too hopeless or too
corrupt to come within its pale, or even to
accept it when they hear it, we must bear it
to them, nay, must press it upon them, and
even compel them to come in. All that the

Saviour meant by this strong expression the Church of God has not yet more than begun to realize. All that tact can do to win them; all that sympathy and consideration for their distress can do to awaken their confidence; and above everything, all that faith can do to bring to bear upon them the constraining power and love of God; all this is implied, and a little of it is illustrated in the Christian philanthropies and blessed agencies of consecrated evangelism in our own and other days. And it is sufficiently vindicated, and has proved effectual from the fact that multitudes of the most honored servants of God, and even the ministers of the Gospel of Jesus Christ, have been snatched from these very ranks; rescued from the very gates of hell; emancipated from both spiritual and literal prisons and chains; miraculously saved from the wreck of drunkenness; pulled out of the seething pollutions of prostitution and saved from the gambling saloon, and bar-room, and pick-pockets' den, to leave behind them the glorious record of a Bunyan, a Newton, or a Jerry McAuley.

THE HEATHEN.

But the last cluster includes a wider circle

than merely the sinful and outcast. These
poor lepers, beyond the pale of the city,
stand for the great heathen world in its helplessness and misery, and the sending out of
the servants to constrain them to come in is
being fulfilled before our eyes in the great
missionary movement of to-day. How solemn the stages represented in this parable.
We have first the rejection of the Gospel by
the children of the kingdom. How perfectly
it fits the picture of Christendom to-day
with the indifference of the great masses in
Christian lands to the message of salvation.
God seems to be at length excusing them
and passing them by for the classes that
have long been regarded as hopeless and
past redemption. And so we have the second stage of the parable: the movement
downward to the slums of the city. Surely
that is going on around us to-day in a most
significant manner.

Finally, there is the third movement beyond the city gates to the great lost masses
of humanity beyond the pale of Christendom. This is the publishing of the "Gospel
of the kingdom as a witness unto all nations," and this is to close the Gospel age
and bring the Master of the feast back

again. How very real all this seems as we
behold it happening before our eyes in these
eventful days.

May God make us faithful to our trust
as His messengers in working in line with
His plan and so hastening His blessed coming.

THE PHARISEE AND PUBLICAN; OR, DIVINE
MERCY IN CONTRAST WITH MAN'S SELF-
RIGHTEOUSNESS.

(Luke xviii. 9-14.)

On the one hand we have the very highest
sample of mere human goodness, in the self-
conscious Pharisee standing in the temple
with head erect, and heart inflated, talking
to himself and about himself and his excellen-
cies, and calling it prayer; so full of self-con-
sciousness that he forgets all about God after
the first breath in which he has pronounced His
name, and becomes in a sort of self-homage
and the contemplation of his own virtues a
god to himself.

"God," and there he parts company with
heaven, "I thank Thee that I am not as
other men are, or even as this publican. I
fast twice in the week, I give tithes of all

that I possess." On the other hand, the poor
sinner stands afar off, feeling himself unworthy even to approach the Pharisee, far
less to lift his eyes to heaven, and simply
confessing his unworthiness, and imploring
the Divine mercy for his own soul, as if
there were no other sinner in the world but
he. "God be merciful to me *the* sinner," is
the real force of the language. There is a
still deeper suggestion in the word he used
for mercy; literally it might be written,
"God be *the propitiation* for me the sinner."
There seems to be the thought of an atonement, of the Divine plan of mercy through
expiation, something that God must arrange,
and that he was helpless to provide, but glad
to accept. Surely this was deepest penitence and simplest faith. Nor need we
wonder that it was instantly effectual. The
very moment he took the sinner's place, and
claimed the sinner's Saviour, he was justified. The Lord Himself emphatically declares that "this man went down to his
house justified." It is a beautiful instance
of the immediate and complete forgiveness
of the soul that takes its true place at the
footstool of mercy. The other went as he
came, satisfied with himself; not needing,

not claiming, not having any part in Christ's salvation.

Ancient legends have left an interesting tradition that strongly resembles this parable, and which Archbishop Trench has used with fine effect. Two men it is said once approached the Master as He passed through the villages of Judea. One of them, a poor sinner, besought His mercy. The other, a robed and phylacteried Pharisee, clasped his hands in holy horror and said, "God grant that I may stand far from this wicked man, in the last day." The Master, it is said, quietly answered: "Both men have their petition. The sinner has asked My mercy, and has obtained it, and in that day, he shall stand on My right hand. The Pharisee has asked that he might stand far from him on that day. His wish is granted, for in the company of redeemed and pardoned sinners he shall never come." The Lord Himself has given us the application in the searching words, "Every one that exalteth himself shall be abased; and he that humbleth himself shall be exalted."

CHAPTER X.

THE PARABLES OF DIVINE MERCY.
(Continued.)

"Likewise I say unto you there is joy in the presence of the angels of God over one sinner that repenteth" (Luke xv. 10).

THE three parables of the fifteenth chapter of Luke are a trinity of Divine love and mercy. Like the Scripture itself, they can not be broken and never should be divided. While each has its separate lesson, they form a glorious unity of truth and grace and a picture of God which is fitted to move and attract every sinner's heart. It is like the photograph which a loving mother, seeking for her long lost daughter, hung up in the dance halls of a great city, hoping that some day her wandering child would see it and come home. So the Son of man has hung up this picture of Divine mercy to attract and win back to God the lost sheep and the wandering prodigals of this sinful world. Let us look first at each of these parables in detail and then seek to gather up the lessons of the series.

9

I.   THE GOOD SHEPHERD, OR THE MERCY OF
      JESUS SEEKING THE LOST.

(Luke xv. 3-7.)

This beautiful picture centers round the
person of Jesus. The sinner is represented
by the foolish sheep, the weakest, most de-
fenceless, and often the most unwise of all
creatures; lost not through wilful intention
always, but through folly, wandering, and
neglect of the shepherd's voice. When lost,
the sheep is the least likely of all creatures
to find itself, and the least able to take care
of itself. "All we, like sheep, have gone
astray. We have turned every one to his
own way." We are represented in the parable as lost in the wilderness. It is a dangerous place, even with the fold around us and
the Shepherd nigh; but without the Shepherd it is a dreadful place to be lost in. Fierce
wolves, trackless wastes, wild tempests, im-
passable torrents, desolate mountains, and
unsheltered wilds;—these are the figures
which portray the misery and perils of lost
souls. The value of the lost one is strangely indicated by the contrast between one
and ninety-nine. Only one was lost, but
that one outweighed all the flock, for the moment of peril and need. Every individual
soul is missed by the Shepherd, and is worth

all His toil and love and suffering. But it
is the picture of the Shepherd that stands
out with most glorious vividness. The moment He discovers that one is lost, He immediately leaves the ninety and nine, and
goes Himself to find it. He does not send
but comes. He seeks the lost one. It tells
of patient love. It tells of His long suffering
pains and toils. It tells of the thirty-three
years of His earthly love and sorrow. It
tells of the long journeys through Galilee
and Judea, the weary summer days, the
sleepless nights, the agony, and bloody
sweat, the denial, the betrayal, the crucifixion, the hideous darkness of the cross, the
hidden face of God, the fierce wolves that
crept upon Him in His dying anguish from
the dark wilderness of His sorrow, the
strange horror of the burden of sin, the love
that has still followed sinful men through
all the years since then; that seeks them
now so patiently, and waits so long to be
gracious, and follows until He finds. And
then when He finds the lost sheep there is
no upbraiding, no scourging; but gently He
lifts it in His bosom; in its weakness, He
carries it along; He does not even feel its
heavy burden; He is so glad to find it that

He carries it on His shoulders, rejoicing;
and when He reaches home, He calls all
heaven to rejoice because the lost is found.
This is the picture of that matchless love,
the seeking, saving, sacrificing, keeping,
overcoming and everlasting love of the Lord
Jesus Christ.

II. THE PARABLE OF THE LOST COIN; OR, THE MERCY OF THE HOLY GHOST.

(Luke xv. 8-10.)

Here the lost soul is represented by the
figure of a coin. This is one of the most familiar symbols of value; and perhaps, the
most expressive to ordinary minds, to whom
nothing seems so valuable as money. The
soul is the precious coin. It still bears upon
it the stamp of God. And although lost
amid rubbish and dust, it still contains the
precious gold, compared with which all other
created things are poor and cheap.

The seeker and finder is a woman; fitting
type of the blessed Comforter, often represented, it would seem, under the image of a
mother. The lost coin is one of the ten
which she has treasured, and for which she
has no doubt a plan of wise investment.

Every one is needed and this lost one cannot be dispensed with. Every soul has its
place in the Divine plan, and is unspeakably
and eternally precious. Until saved and restored, it is out of its true place, and something is lost in the full purpose of God. Like
this woman, the Holy Spirit is the great
seeker of lost souls. For eighteen hundred
years the Divine Comforter has been thus
engaged, seeking in dark corners and un-
clean recesses for the immortal treasures
which man has thrown away.

The process of the search is instructive and
expressive. The lighting of the candle suggests
the work of spiritual illumination, the shining
in of the truth upon the conscience and heart,
the quickening of our spiritual apprehensions
and convictions, the revealing to the soul,
of sin and God. The sweeping of the house
has also its counterpart in the dealings of
God with souls under conviction, the sharp
and sudden trials that come, the knock of
sickness, bereavement, disappointment, or
loss, upon the door of the closed heart, the
shaking up of our circumstances, until we
are compelled to look around us and realize
our situation, and awake to the consciousness of our danger. And all through this,

the Spirit is seeking diligently, whispering
to the heart, touching every chord of
impression and aspiration, and drawing the
soul to Jesus. How long the process sometimes lasts and how patiently the blessed
Spirit waits till He finds the lost coin; and
then the joy of the Holy Ghost over the new
found heart. This is the secret of the strange
gladness that comes into the soul when truly
converted. It is the joy of the Spirit overflowing into the consciousness of the sinner,
until it becomes his joy, too.

III. THE PARABLE OF THE PRODIGAL SON; OR,
THE MERCY OF THE FATHER.

(Luke xv. 18-32.)

First, we see the picture of the sinner.
What selfishness. "Give me! give me! the
portion that falleth to me." What earthli-
ness of desire; the portion of goods, the
things that I can eat and drink, and wear,
and enjoy with my senses. What self-will
and false independence of control! He only
longs to get away from the restraints of authority, to be his own free master, only to
find at last that he has become a slave.

What heartlessness, and alienation from

his Father's love! He goes as far as he can from his home, and suffers no thought of compunction for the father's feelings, or consideration for a father's love.

What profligacy and riotous living! He wasted his substance; spent all. How myriads of young men to-day are just wasting their strength and life, expending their God-given powers in the exhaustion and self-destruction of base indulgence.

What misery at last! "A mighty famine." "He began to be in want." "He had spent all." How soon the cup of pleasure is drained. How soon even our own natures refuse even to reward indulgence with delight. How soon lust ends in satiety and disgust; and that which administered pleasure becomes a stinging pain and torture. Not even the husks of the swine are afforded him. There comes a time when even the basest and coarsest gratifications lose their power to please, and the soul feels that it is starving; and even if surrounded with everything in the universe it would seem to be perishing of hunger.

What shame and disgrace! "He joined himself to a citizen of that country who sent him into his fields to feed swine." He is a poor slave of Satan, and the devil uses him only for the meanest purposes. How many men that might have been useful to-day, and honorable, if they had only obeyed the Father's commands, and trusted the Father's love, are pouring out alcoholic swill to feed the filthy swine that swarm the bar-room, and yet themselves unable to take any pleasure from it, and living a life of constant torment and self-reproach, because of their wasted youth and opportunities.

And finally, how complete the wreck! "When he came to himself." It looks as if even reason had been dethroned. The sinner is a madman and a fool. And when he comes to himself, he feels as one that is awakened from a dream of insane delusion and desperate folly.

HIS REPENTANCE AND RETURN.

The first step was his coming to himself. It suggests the first moment of reflection. At length, after the wild rush of years, he stops for a moment and begins to think. It is the first pause of his headlong heart, since he left his father's home. Oh, if souls would only think, God could speak to them, and mercy could still reach them.

The next strand in the cord of love that at length brought him home, was the thought of his father. "In my father's house is bread enough and to spare." It is the thought of God's love and grace that always prompts true repentance.

Next is the question of his own misery. "I perish with hunger." At length he realizes his true situation, and is willing to confess to himself his failure and misery. And everything that he has called pleasure and freedom, he sees at last to be a cruel mockery and a hideous dream.

And then comes that which must always accompany any true return, the purpose of his will. "I will arise and go to my father." If men would only realize that their choices and purposes are the true helms of life! Any one can be saved who simply wills it.

Then comes the spirit of humility, penitence, and readiness to confess his fault. "I will say unto him, Father, I have sinned." There is nothing degrading in a sincere confession. There is nothing more manly and noble than an honorable apology for a mistake; and penitence is simply a becoming apology to our glorious and gracious Parent, and is necessary for our own true self-respect, as well as for any just or lasting pardon.

And yet with all this, there was much that was wrong in the spirit and repentance of the prodigal. There was much of pride still lingering in his heart, and he was really determined to buy his way back to his father's favor; or, at least, to earn some place as a servant at his board. It was a self-righteous idea which always clings to the fallen heart. I will do something to deserve God's mercy. "I will say to my father, Father, I have sinned and am no more worthy to be called thy son." This is all right; but, "make me one of thy hired servants," is the very self-righteousness which Christ and His apostles declared shut the Pharisees out of the Kingdom of Heaven. It is the sinner still comforting himself with the thought that he is going to do better, and somehow make up for his past misdeeds by trying to serve God. Happily, when he got back, his father choked all this out of him before he was able to utter it. He let him say, "I have sinned and am no more worthy to be called thy son," and then he stopped short all the rest of his studied speech by his overflowing welcome, and his fatherly reconciliation. Therefore, although our penitence may be imperfect, and our faith be weak and faltering, let us come the best we can. This is the beautiful teaching of this parable, and it comes out with still more force in the next division.

HIS RECEPTION AND RECONCILIATION.

First, it was immediate. The father did not wait until he got back, and stood in the reception room and made an ample apology; but before he heard a word from his lips; when he saw him in the distance, and still a great way off, he ran to meet him, and, without a particle of reserve, manifested by his actions his overflowing welcome and forgiving love. So God meets on the way the first desire and endeavor of the penitent soul to return to Him, and even before we are conscious of the truth in its Divine clearness, somehow, our heart has been made to feel that He is ready to receive us graciously, and love us freely.

Next, it was cordial and gracious. "He had compassion. He ran and fell on his neck and kissed him." It was not only a gracious acquittal, but a full hearty forgiveness. When God saves a sinner He does

not merely tolerate him, but He loves him
with all His heart.

Further, it was not only gracious, but it
was free. No word of any conditions was
suffered. As we have seen, the ungenerous
speech which the son had meditated, offering to pay his way, or earn his living as a
servant, was not allowed to be uttered; but,
by the father's free, unconditional mercy, he
was welcomed and perfectly restored. So
the sinner is received, not because of the
service he is going to render, not because of
the love he is going to show, not because of
the value he is going to prove; but absolute-
ly and wholly through the Divine mercy, and
for the sake of the atoning sacrifice of the
Lord Jesus Christ, our perfect Ransom and
our only plea.

Again, it was paternal. The father would
not suffer him to be a servant, or anything
else than a very child. And so he immediately commands that the symbol of sonship
shall be put upon him, the best robe, the
ring of affection, the shoes of dignity, the
feast of honor, and the assurance, "This my
son is alive again. My lost one is found."
And so the soul that returns to Christ can
not go half way, and can not stay in the

kitchen, and in the fields of servile bondage. There is only one place, and that is in the Father's arms, and at the Father's table. Nothing less than complete sonship is provided or permitted for the most vile and unworthy of God's ransomed ones.

Marvelous grace, unspeakable dignity! This moment reeking in sin, clothed in rags; the next, seated in honor and purity as heirs of God and joint heirs with Christ, and saying with rapturous wonder, "Behold what manner of love the Father hath bestowed upon us that we should be called the sons of God." The best robe expressed perfect justification, and Divine holiness. The ring is the token of covenant love. The shoes are marks of honor; slaves always walked with naked feet. The feast tells of the joy and gladness to which God receives His restored children. And the Father's word proclaims how mighty the transformation, how terrible the ruin, and how literally the salvation of the soul is life from the dead.

CONCLUSION.

The first lesson which we are taught by this series of parables is the preciousness of the human soul. This is presented under th image of a lost sheep which was almost as dear as a child to an Oriental shepherd; of a lost coin, which with many people is the supreme standard of value, and of a lost son, which is the climax of all that the human heart holds dear. The lost soul is as dear to God as the sheep to its tender shepherd; the precious treasure to the men and women who make it the supreme object of their life, and the fondly loved child for whom a father or mother would give all the world. Still further there is a heightening scale of value and appreciation shown in the parables in the fact that in the first it is one out of a hundred that is lost; in the second it is one out of ten, but in the third it is one out of two, intimating that when God lost the human race He lost one-half of the things of value in this entire universe.

The next lesson we are taught is the love of God for sinners. The whole Trinity is revealed here in the fulness of Divine love. The parable of the prodigal son tells of the love of the Father. The parable of the good shepherd tells of the love of the Son. The parable of the woman tells of the love of the Holy Ghost. Father, Son and Holy Ghost

are all working and waiting to save the lost
sinner if he will only come.

There is a strange and touching picture
here of the heavenly world and its interest
in the salvation of men. What efforts men
have made through the telescope to get one
little glimpse of yonder worlds of space.
How poor the light that even the finest telescope sheds on those celestial realms. But
Christ has given us here one glimpse of
heaven at the very moment when the tidings
arrive that a lost son has been found. All
heaven is overcome with joy; the angels rejoice, the Father rejoices, the Son rejoices,
the Holy Ghost rejoices. God is not ashamed
to show His joy "in the presence of the angels," and there are other beings that rejoice
still more. There is the mother whose last
message was one of loving appeal that you
should turn to God. There is the wife who
walked by your side and whose beckoning
hands are calling you to come home. There
is the little child that left the gates ajar for
you to follow. Oh, the tender, sacred cords
that are drawing sinners home.

The next lesson is what we might call
the theology of salvation. The writer was
once asked by a Unitarian why men could

not be saved by the parable of the prodigal son and what need there was for all this talk about the atonement in view of the picture Christ Himself has given us of the Father's love and willingness to save. The Holy Spirit immediately suggested the answer. "The parable of the son is not complete in itself, but follows the parable of the good shepherd. The father could not welcome his lost child back until first the shepherd, by his sufferings, opened the way. The three parables together constitute the Gospel message. The Saviour must suffer and die; the Spirit must seek and find and then the sinner comes home and the Father welcomes him to His heart."

The part of the sinner in the process of salvation is made very plain here. First: he must see his condition, his misery, his sin and come to himself. Next he must resolve and choose to return to God. It is not "I feel," but "I will" that turns the scale. "I will arise; I will go to my father." The salvation of every soul is a matter for his individual choice. It is simply making up your mind and then going. Then, of course, there is repentance. "I have sinned. I am not worthy to be called thy son." There is noth-

ing more honorable on the part of a gentleman than a manly apology for his fault. Repentance is just an honorable acknowledg-
ment to God that we are wrong and a fixed
purpose to change our way and turn from
our sin.

Finally, we have an humbling view at the
close of the last parable of something worse
even than the sinner's sin, namely: the
uncharitableness of the older brother who
refused to join in the welcome to the prodigal and threw the shadow of his selfishness
across that happy scene. He had his punishment in being shut out from the festival
by his own spirit. Yes, the worst of all sins
is the sin of lovelessness. God save us from
the curse of religious selfishness and give to
us the spirit of Him who came to "seek and
to save that which was lost."

CHAPTER XI.

THE PARABLES OF HUMAN DESTINY.

THE four parables which we group together in this chapter present a striking view of human destiny. The first represents the destiny of the worldling in this life, up to the hour of death; the second, the fruitless professor, up to the close of life; the third, the use of present opportunities to prepare for eternal destiny; and the fourth, the contrasted destiny of the worldling and the saint in time and eternity.

THE RICH FOOL.

(Luke xii. 16-21.)

This parable represents the character and destiny of the man of the world, up to the close of the present life. How vividly we see in this picture the restless, grasping spirit of avarice, of seeking to add to its possessions, and seemingly unsatisfied with all its gains. Even more emphatically the picture reveals the godlessness of worldliness. He omits from all his plans the very thought of God, or His sovereign will and omnipotent control of our

very life, and all we can call our own. "This
will I do. I will pull down my barns and will
build greater. I will say to my soul, Soul,
thou has much goods stored up for many
years." The first mention of God in the parable is when He steps in upon the scene, and
the two short words, "But God," turn to confusion, and dissolve to nothingness all the vain
and self-sufficient plans of human selfishness.

We see also in this miserable worldling the
utter selfishness of the spirit of the world.
While there is no grateful recognition of God,
or thought of pleasing or serving Him, neither
is there any desire or purpose to use His
wealth for the happiness and good of others.
He regarded it as all his own, and he proposed
to enjoy it by himself and for himself. "Thou
hast much goods, take thine ease; eat, drink
and be merry." He had taught his soul no
higher pleasure than that which sensuality affords, and fed its immortal needs on things
of earthly nature. There is nothing said about
his vices or crimes. He is simply a worldling:
seeking and successfully finding for a time, his
portion in the things of earth, and binding
them to his bosom as his idols, his ends, and
his supreme enjoyments, with no sense of God,
and no regard for higher obligations, either

to his Maker, or to his fellow man.—How terrible, even here, the issue of such a life; the sudden summons of the last inevitable messenger; the awful disappointment at the loss of every earthly thing; the fearful message of a God that he has never recognized or loved; the irresistible separation of his soul from all its treasures, and its naked and terrified appearance before the eternal tribunal; and the bitter consciousness that all he has labored for, and hoped to enjoy, is to pass to others, who shall, perhaps, not even thank him; and to be irretrievably lost and forever, to him, and to all the higher ends for which he might have consecrated them. It is a lost life, all the more terrific, because he had so much to lose. Some one has sarcastically remarked of such a man at his death, "How much has he left?" and the answer, bitter as wormwood, and hopeless as despair is, "He has left all." He had nothing but his gold, and with the loss of that, he has nothing left. Dr. Johnson once said to his friends, as he looked at the wealth and splendor of an earthly estate, "Ah, Boswell, these are the things that make death terrible."

The vision does not pass in through the curtains that hide the future. Just a momentary glance we get that indicates the desolate spirit passing beyond, and casting one lingering look of horror on all that he has lost and left behind. But the eternal side is reserved for the later parables. Enough for the present that we fully realize the earthly wreck and the mortal side of the sad picture; the desolation and despair of the soul that has invested everything in Mammon, and finds his house of sand collapse in a moment in ruin and despair. The parable is chiefly intended to show the utter transitoriness of earthly things; the certainty and suddenness of their loss; the bitter disappointment which their loss will bring; the folly and shortsightedness of those who have no other treasure and hope; and the wickedness of those who, as the Lord expressed it, live to lay up treasure only for themselves, and are not rich toward God. At the same time there is a solemn intimation of the life beyond for which the soul has made no provision, where it must eternally reap the consequences of its shortsightedness and sin.

THE BARREN FIG TREE; OR, THE DESTINY OF THE FRUITLESS PROFESSOR AS SEEN EVEN HERE.

(Luke xiii. 6-9.)

While the rich fool represents the worldling,

the fruitless fig tree represents the nominal
Christian, as well as the Jewish nation for
whom, of course, it was primarily intended. It
is not enough that we should be planted in His
vineyard, and even watered by His grace and
care. The only ultimate test of reality and
ripeness is fruit. Long the husbandman bears
with the empty branches. Patiently he waits,
and seeks by careful culture to cherish the de-
caying life, and save the fruitless tree from de-
struction. Lovingly the interceding Saviour
pleads for the faithless one, and renews the influences of His grace and spirit; digging about
its roots by trial, and seeking to fertilize them
by the influences of truth, and the blessed Holy
Spirit. But at last there is a limit, and even
the Saviour will plead no more. Love must
not betray itself by displacing and injuring
others for the sake of one that will not improve
its opportunities. The fruitless tree cumber-
eth the ground; and not only wastes the soil
and the space of the vineyard, but disfigures it,
overshadows others, and brings reproach upon
the husbandman; and so at last, the word goes
forth, "Cut it down"; and the intercessor
raises no pleading voice against the fatal blow.

So Jerusalem was cut down in the days of
the captivity. So again, the fruitless tree that

Jesus and His disciples so patiently labored to
nourish into life and fruition, fell before the
Roman armies. So the Master threatened the
churches of Pergamos, Thyatira, Sardis and
Laodicea, with His judgment stroke. And so
each individual soul that proves faithless to its
trust, neglects its opportunities, and wastes
the rich grace of a loving Saviour in selfishness
and negligence, shall be put aside from the
place of privilege and opportunity, and summoned to the judgment of the unprofitable
servant. How solemnly, sometimes, comes the
stroke of death to the unfaithful Christian.
And although perhaps, the soul may not be
hopelessly lost, yet it is dragged away with the
awful sense of lost opportunities, neglected
truths, forfeited rewards, and the disapproval
at last of the Master to whom it had pledged
its undivided love and service. How sad and
bitter the departing cry,

> "Must I go, and empty handed,
>   Must I meet my Saviour so?"
> And how wise the solemn question,
>   "And shall I thus the Master meet,
>   And at the awful judgment seat,
> Bring nought but withered leaves?"

THE PRUDENT STEWARD; OR, THE WISE USE OF
PRESENT OPPORTUNITY, TO PREPARE FOR
FUTURE DESTINY.

(Luke xvi. 1-12.)

This is a very remarkable parable, requiring
delicacy of discrimination in interpreting it so
as to avoid confusion and error. The steward,
in this case, had been guilty of unfaithfulness
in his trust, and in consequence was about to
be dismissed, and lose his present home and
situation. But at the last moment, finding his
impending danger, he displayed a spirit of remarkable prudence and forethought in taking
advantage of his remaining days of opportunity to make provision for the future, and secure
friends and a home when he should be turned
out of his present situation. We are told that
the Lord commended the unjust steward because he had acted wisely. This does not mean
that the Lord Jesus commended him; the lord
who commended him was his own master
whom he had already defrauded, and now so
shrewdly outwitted; he could not help acknow-
ledging the smartness of the fellow, in making
the most of his situation to provide for the
future. Even men of the world can appreciate
shrewdness in the man that victimizes them.

The Lord Jesus does not commend his injustice, but He takes occasion from his prudence to teach us a lesson of the importance of using our little while of time and opportunity, to prepare for the destinies of the future.

We, like this steward, have been given a great and solemn trust. Like him also, we have been unfaithful to it, and are about to be called to account. The time is coming when each of us shall have to pass out of our present habitations, into the uncertain future; but mercy still suspends the execution of the sentence for a little while. The bailiff death has not yet knocked at our door; and until he does, there is an opportunity for doing something to provide for the time when we shall be houseless and homeless. We can use the present life for this great end, to prepare for the future, so that when we are driven away from this earthly tabernacle, there shall be friends waiting up yonder to receive us into everlasting habitations. This is what the Saviour means by making friends of the Mammon of unrighteousness. That is, so to use the world, that when we shall leave it we shall have gotten out of it something that shall abide forever; shall have so improved the opportunities of grace and salvation; so consecrated and turned to

divine account even the money, the friendships,
and the secular business of life, that we shall
have treasure laid up in heaven, and the loss
of earth will be infinitely compensated by the
everlasting gain. It is the same teaching which
the Lord has elsewhere given in His Sermon
on the Mount: "Lay up for yourselves treasures in heaven where neither moth nor rust
corrupt, nor thieves break through and steal."
It is the idea the apostle repeats to Timothy in
his letter: "Charge them that are rich in this
world, that they be not highminded, nor trust
in uncertain riches, but in the living God, who
giveth us richly all things to enjoy; that they
do good, that they be rich in good works, ready
to distribute, willing to communicate; laying
up in store for themselves a good foundation
against the time to come, that they may lay
hold on eternal life." Of course it does not
mean that either money or the consecrated use
of money will save us. But it does mean that
we can use our opportunities of life and grace
to accept the salvation of the Lord Jesus. And
then we can so turn to account our means, our
business, and our entire life in loving service
for Christ, that there *shall be reserved for us*
through His grace, an everlasting recompense,
and a better and enduring substance.

This parable then, is a link between the ones that precede it, and those that follow. The two former refer to human destiny in the present life, or rather, at death. This looks on to the eternity beyond, and teaches us to so use the present even notwithstanding our failures and sins, as to prepare for it, and lay up treasure in it.

THE RICH MAN AND LAZARUS; OR, THE DESTINY OF UNFAITHFUL SOULS AFTER DEATH.

(Luke xvi. 19-31.)

This remarkable and most solemn picture carries us forward from the present, to the eternal world, and reveals the judgments and recompenses which await each individual at the close of the present life.

First, we have the picture of two lives in vivid contrast. The one is a man who has everything that this world can afford without God. He is not necessarily a wicked man in the common sense of that word; he is simply a worldly man without God. His portion is purely earthly; but it is complete as such a portion can be. He is rich and lives in luxury, and every indulgence. His taste and vanity are gratified by the most elegant and costly apparel. His sensual appetites are ministered to by every form of physical gratification. He dwells in a splendid mansion, and no doubt is surrounded by a retinue of servants, and a circle of admiring friends; and perhaps, has all that affection can add to the more refined enjoyments of life; but that is all.

The other is a man that has nothing that the world values. He is a poor diseased beggar, without the means even of obtaining his necessary food, except through the charity of this very rich man; and without a friend to minister to his sufferings, except the dogs that licked his sores. It is the uttermost contrast of earthly conditions. But as the one compensation, he has God, and the hope of heaven. This is not intended to glorify poverty, or to depreciate wealth; but simply to show how little the world is worth without God, and how much God is worth without the world.

Next, we have the picture of death. To both of these men it comes. To the rich man it comes with all the pomp and splendor of his condition. No doubt the wisest physicians attended him; and the widest sympathy cheered and encouraged his closing days; but none of them could keep the grim messenger away. And when he died he was buried. This is emphatic. No doubt he had a costly and splendid funeral. Multitudes of mourners. Sublimest music. The grandest state. And perhaps, a tomb that tried to make death seem only a splendid pageant; and the narrow house, the palace of magnificence. The beggar died too, but perhaps, was not even buried. If he was, the public wagon hustled his uncoffined bones to the pauper's field, where no headstone marked his resting place, and no tear was ever shed above his forgotten dust.

And so the first two scenes close, and Dives seems to have all the advantage. But now the next scene opens. It is eternity. How instantly and awfully all is changed. The narrative changes too. The beggar now comes to the front, and is first described, as he had the last place in the previous pictures. What procession of celestial forms is this we see swiftly and triumphantly passing through the fields of air, and entering the heavenly portals? This is the beggar's funeral procession. But it is not death, but life, he is entering. He is carried by angels into Abraham's bosom. At the very head of the table; and reclining as in ancient feasts, so that his head would rest on the shoulder of the very Master of the supper, he sits down, and "shall hunger no more, neither thirst any more," or ever say again, "I am sick." It is not necessary to dwell on all the details of the heavenly picture. It looks a little like the Old Testament paradise just before the ascension of Jesus opened heaven to all believers. It was perhaps the happy home of saved ones before Jesus came. It was not the final heaven, but the blessed home of the waiting ones, under the Abrahamic covenant, who were resting with their fathers until the Lord Jesus should open the portals of heaven to all believers. But it is enough that it was home, and rest, and happiness, and all of heaven that he could then enjoy.

And now, we turn to the other side. What an awful picture! "In hell," is the first vivid coloring on the canvas. "In torment" is the next. "In this flame," is the lurid light that next flashes upon the scene. "A single drop of water to cool my tongue," is the bitter cry. Abraham afar off, and Lazarus in his bosom, is the sight of heaven which adds a million fold to the bitterness of hell. And last of all, "a great gulf fixed so that they that would pass from us to you cannot; and neither can they pass from you to us." There is no transition there. No second probation. No hope of reprieve or change.

"But fixed the doom of all remains
And everlasting silence reigns."

There seems a strange consciousness still of earth. A vivid memory of all the past, and a clear sense now of the madness and folly of his earthly choice, with a strange desire to save his brethren from his terrific fate. But even that is impossible; and his own anguish is enhanced by the horrible fear that his bad example has ruined others as well as himself; and that in a little while he shall see their sufferings, too, which he can less easily bear than his own. Is this then the punishment of wealth? No, but it is the loss of eternal life, and the neglect of heaven for the sake of the present world. And it is designed to illustrate the Master's oft repeated message, "What shall it profit a man if he gain the whole world, and lose his own soul?" And again, "Seek ye first the Kingdom of God and His righteousness, and all things shall be added unto you." "It is better to enter into life halt and maimed having one eye than having two eyes to be cast into hell where their worm dieth not, and their fire is not quenched."

One lesson more should be added—namely, that our immortal destiny is settled not by our social condition, but by our faith and obedience with reference to the Word of God. The final answer of Abraham to this wretched spirit in the depths of despair implies, that the cause of his and his brethren's ruin was, that they had refused to hear Moses and the prophets; and that not even the miracle of his return from the dead would be effectual, and lead to their faith and repentance. The ground of human destiny is our treatment of God and His Word. "He that believeth shall be saved, and he that believeth not shall be damned." "He that heareth these sayings of mine and doeth them, I will liken him unto a wise man, which built his house upon a rock: And the rain descended, and the floods came, and the winds blew, and beat upon that house; and it fell not: for it was founded upon a rock. And everyone that heareth these sayings of mine, and doeth them not, shall be likened unto a foolish man, which built his house upon the sand: And the rain descended, and the floods came, and the winds blew, and beat upon that house; and it fell: and great was the fall of it."

CHAPTER XII.

THE PARABLES OF HUMAN DESTINY

(Continued).

PARABLE OF THE UNJUST JUDGE AND THE POUNDS.

THESE two parables present a double picture of human destiny, first in relation to the church of Christ and secondly in relation to the individual believer. The parable of the Unjust Judge is a picture of the church in her conflict with the adversary, waiting for the coming of the Lord. The parable of the Pounds represent the ministry of Christ's servants under the dispensation of the Holy Spirit and in view of the coming of Christ.

THE UNJUST JUDGE.

(Luke xviii. 1-8.)

1. The Widow. There was in a city a certain widow. This widow represents the church of Christ. While she is the Bride of the Lamb, yet the Bridegroom is now absent and she is alone and exposed to the hatred and opposition of her great adversary, the devil.

2. The Adversary. We know who this is.

11

From the beginning, the wicked one has sought
to destroy the church of Christ. He is represented in the book of Revelation as a dragon
waiting to devour her seed.

3. The Recourse. She appeals to God in
prayer. Indeed, the specific lesson of the parable as represented in the opening verse is that
"Men ought always to pray and not to faint."
She is represented as "crying unto God day and
night." This is our best defense against every
form of opposition and trial. This is our best
weapon in our warfare of work for God and
men. The church needs to learn afresh the
power of collective prayer, united prayer and
prayer as a real business that takes hold of
God and expects Him to do real things for us.

4. A Picture of God. He is here presented
in contrast with the unjust judge. We are
not to suppose that we need to worry Him by
our importunity into granting petitions as this
woman worried the indifferent magistrate into
listening to her plea. The whole figure here
is one of antithesis. The unjust judge is in
contrast with God and the Lord Jesus asks,
"Shall not God avenge His own elect which
cry unto Him day and night, though He bear
long with them? I tell you He will avenge
them speedily." In contrast with the earthly

official, He will not keep them waiting but will promptly and gladly respond to their appeal.

There is a fine suggestion in the figure of the judge full of encouragement for our prayers. God is not only a Father loving to help His children; not only a God of mercy and love willing to bless because of His goodness and grace, but we have claims upon Him on the grounds of righteousness as a judge. We do not come to Him in prayer as mendicants to beg a pittance for which we have no claim, but we approach Him as the counsellor at law approaches the judge of the court and pleads the statutes of the commonwealth and the claims of equity and asks for his client judgment not as a charity but as a right. Our great Advocate, the Lord Jesus Christ, has established our rights before the throne of prayer and has presented an equivalent for all that we can ask from heaven, so that in His name we are entitled to ask the largest things, to present our strong reasons; to bring our prevailing plea and to know that God is not only merciful but also "faithful and just to forgive us our sins and cleanse us from all unrighteousness."

5. The Cause of Failure. Why then, do we not receive more frequent and valuable an-

swers to our prayers? The Lord Himself gives
the reason. "When the Son of man cometh
shall He find faith on the earth?" It is the lack
of faith. It is the spirit of unbelief. And so
the great lesson of the parable comes in with
"Men ought always to pray and not to faint."
The word "always" does not mean that we are
to pray under all circumstances and at all
times, but we are to pray through. We are
not to stop until we receive our petition. We
are not to be discouraged by delay or faint because of the extreme conditions of our case,
but we are to "come boldly to the throne of
grace" and "pray with all perseverance."

6. The final lesson of the parable, however,
teaches the great thought of future destiny.
The real deliverance of the widow is to come
when her Bridegroom comes. "When the Son
of man cometh"—this is the outlook of the suffering church and the waiting age. Then all
wrongs shall be righted. Then the cruel adversary will be found and cast out. Then the
Bride of the Lamb shall shine more glorious
than the sun and share through the coming
ages the throne and kingdom of her Lord. Is
this our blessed hope and are we "looking for
and hasting forward" that glorious day?

THE PARABLE OF THE POUNDS.

(Luke xix. 12-27.)

This parable has reference, not to the church, but to the individual believer in view of the coming of the Master.

1. His Going Away. "A certain nobleman went into a far country to receive for himself a kingdom." Christ has gone into heaven and there are gathering one by one the members of His future kingdom and preparing for that glorious age when He and His people shall together reign over earth and heaven.

2. His Commission to His Servants. He left His earthly interests in the hands of His servants. While He represents us yonder, we are to represent Him here. We have charge of His affairs and stand for the interests of His kingdom on earth.

3. Their Enduement for Service. He gave to each of them a pound. We will notice the difference between the parable of the pounds and the talents. In the latter case, they received different investments; one five, another two and another one. In this case they all received alike. The talents seem to refer to God's special gifts to His people, the pounds to the one great gift of the Holy Ghost. Our

one great equipment for service is the Spirit
of Pentecost. Without Him we can do no
work for God effectually, either in the home,
the church or the closet. He gives the one
Spirit to each of His servants. The differ-
ences among Christian workers are not due to
favoritism or partiality on the part of God, but
to the different way in which each follower of
Christ improves His gift. We all have the
same opportunity of claiming and using the
divine power and our supernatural equipment
for the work committed to our hands. We do
not need many gifts but one, and that one is
comprehensive of all others. The Holy Ghost
is wisdom, power, holiness, faith, love, prayer,
everything a Christian worker can require, all
comprehended in the one living Presence that
comes to abide in the heart that is yielded
wholly to Him. Have we received this divine
equipment and are we keeping the fire burning
and "stirring up the gift of God that is in us?"

4. The Use and Improvement of this Divine
Enduement. "Occupy till I come." This
word "occupy" means to use. We are to be
active in employing the gifts of the Spirit for
the work of God, and as we do so, the gift will
grow and our pound will become ten pounds.
This appears to be the meaning of the apostle

in the twelfth chapter of First Corinthians, "The manifestation of the Spirit is given to every man to profit withal." This profiting is a commercial phrase. We are to use our divine gifts as the business man uses his capital and his investments. This explains the difference between different Christians. The one has been more faithful and diligent in the use of his resources and they have multiplied. George Mueller used to say that after years of experience of God's faithfulness it was as easy for him to ask and receive thousands as it was pounds. Oh, that it might be true of us as of the early Christians, "Your faith groweth exceedingly!" "Being fruitful in every good work and increasing in the knowledge of God."

5. The Master's Return. At length He comes. This is the goal of Christian hope and longing desire. He has waited long, but He will come. He is already on the way. The signs of His appearing are on every hand. Oh, how glad the prospect and yet how solemn its significance!

6. The Accounting. His coming means our accountability to God and His reckoning with us for our life work and our eternal reward. This is not the judgment of the Great White Throne, the day of wrath and doom. This is

the Judgment Seat of Christ where His own servants are to have passed in review their earthly work, and to receive according to what they have done and be assigned their places in the coming kingdom. This was the great motive of the apostle in all his ministry. He was ever looking forward to that time when he should present his work and receive his crown.

And so the servants come before Him with their several accounts. The first two servants have a happy reckoning. They have wisely used the trust committed to them and multiplied their pound, the one ten-fold, the other five-fold, and their recompense is first the commendation of their Lord and secondly a higher trust and a nobler service. The reward is proportioned to the measure of service rendered. For every pound, there is a city in the empire of the skies. The reward is distinguished honor and noble employ. The heaven of the Bible is no luxurious sinecure, but the most glorious activity. The work we have loved to do below will be continued with nobler capacities and larger scope through the ages to come. The philanthropist, the missionary, the benefactor of his fellowmen, the consecrated genius shall all have congenial work, but on a higher plane and with unbounded resources and the

glorious addition that there will be no night to
close the working day and no dark grave to
cut short the story. The whole creation will be
the empire of our high dominion and the the-
atre of our eternal employ. How inspiring the
prospect! How sublime the vision! How uplifting the motive which it gives to us in all our
ministries now! We are but apprentices preparing for the manhood of the future and the
sovereignty of the ages to come.

But there was one servant who had no such
object or reward. He simply brought his
pound carefully wrapped up in a napkin and
carefully preserved but utterly unimproved.
He had done nothing with his trust. That was
all. But the reason which he gives shows how
wrong his heart had been and reveals the secret
of all our failures in the sight of God. "I
feared thee," he said, "that thou art an austere
man; thou takest up that thou layest not
down and reapest that thou didst not sow."
He had wrong views of his master. He did
not know God. He did not love Him. He
did not trust Him, and of course there was
no incentive to serve Him. Nothing but the
love of Christ can inspire true service, and if
we are coming short, it is because we do not
know the love of God. What a surprise it

must have been to him when he saw at last the glorious recompenses of his fellow-servants, and how he wished, no doubt, that he could live his life once more, and how we will wish some time that we had better understood the generous heart of our great Master and had better used the capital which He had entrusted to our hands! The punishment of this faithless servant was the loss of the blessing he had received. The pound was taken from him and given to the one that had used his trust more wisely. Neglect and unfaithfulness rob us of what we have. If we are not growing, we are retrograding. If we are not revolving on our axles in the busy mechanism of life, we are rusting and preparing for the refuse heap and the dumping cart. There is no intimation of any other judgment upon this unfaithful servant than the rebuke of his master and the loss of his pound. There is a very clear distinction between the unfaithful servant and "Those Mine enemies who would not that I should reign over them." The "enemies" are slain. The faithless servant is deposed. There is the judgment of loss for the unfaithful Christian, but it is very different from the judgment of perdition that awaits the wicked.

Both are sad enough, but the latter is irretrievable.

The two most solemn lessons which this parable teaches us are:

1. Our power for service must all come from God and He has given to us all the equipment necessary for His work. The Holy Ghost is our enduement and He is given to every child of God who will give Him right of way and yield himself to His direction and control. This makes our responsibility for service very great. We cannot plead our incompetency. We cannot excuse ourselves because of our inability. He is not asking us to do more, but to take more from Him.

2. Our Accountability and Liberty.

Daniel Webster used to say that the most stupendous thought that ever came to him was man's accountability to God. It seems to us that this thought will be heightened very much when we combine with it the other thought of our personal liberty in view of our accountability to do with our lives as we will. God is not continually policing our life and pursuing us with detectives every step of our way, but He is quietly letting us alone and saying to each one of us, "Occupy till I come," and each of us is living our life ourselves in view of that

great and solemn day. If we want to be selfish,
we can. If we allow opportunities to pass by,
we may. No lightning stroke will fall upon us.
No outward pressure may be brought to bear.
We are left to the motives and impulses of our
own hearts and meanwhile the phonograph of
the skies is recording silently, constantly, every
act and influence of our lives for the day of
reckoning. Then will come the review and
the recompense or retribution. Oh, how
solemn it is to have such liberty and such accountability! God help us to keep it in view.

"Oh, that each in the day of His coming may say
I have fought my way through,
I have finished the work Thou didst give me to do."

CHAPTER XIII.

THE SON OF MAN AND SICKNESS.

"And ought not this woman, being a daughter of
Abraham, whom Satan hath bound, lo, these eighteen years, be loosed from this bond on the Sabbath
day?" (Luke xiii. 16).

THE miracle recorded in this chapter is
peculiar to Luke and it sheds much
light upon the subject of Divine healing and the ministry of our Lord to the sick
and suffering. Among the special teachings
we may gather from it may be mentioned:

THE RELATION OF SATAN TO DISEASE.

Our first introduction to this woman points
to a deeper cause for her trouble than mere
physical conditions. It is said she had "a
spirit of infirmity." There is no doubt about
what this means. A demon power had taken
possession of her body and bound her limbs
so that "she could in no wise lift up herself."
We must not carry this too far by concluding
that all sickness comes directly from Satanic
power. Sickness may come from a physical
cause and it may come from the direct stroke
of God Himself in judgment. We read that

"the Lord struck the child that Uriah's wife bare unto David and it was very sick." But that it is often the result of demon power, there can be no question if we are to believe the words of the Lord Himself. In this case an evil spirit had taken control of the limbs of this helpless cripple and bound her hand and foot for eighteen years. This does not at all imply that she was a bad woman or under the control of the wicked one in her spirit and life. On the contrary, she is expressly described as "a daughter of Abraham" and was evidently regarded by the Lord as a true servant of God. Satan may and does afflict God's children even as of old he inflicted on Job his loathsome boils and later tried to hinder Paul in his work in a similar way. The realization of this fact ought to be a powerful incentive to us in claiming healing and refusing to be disabled and defiled by the touch of our hated adversary.

Let us arise and repel his power and the Lord will come to our aid as He did to hers. Submission to sickness is not always submission to God, but often to God's enemy and ours, and the exhortation is as applicable to our bodies as to our spirits "Resist the devil and he will flee from you."

THE RELATION OF DIVINE HEALING TO THE VERY IMPULSES OF HUMANITY.

The Lord appeals to the sentiment of human compassion even for a suffering brute and asks "Doth not each one of you on the Sabbath loose his ox or his ass and lead him away to watering and ought not this woman to be loosed from this bond on the Sabbath day?" Surely, God is not less pitiful than human compassion and on the very lowest grounds of humanity we may expect Him to meet the needs of our physical life as well as of our higher nature.

SICKNESS AND THE WILL OF GOD.

We know of no stronger statement of the Lord's willingness, nay more, the Lord's will to heal His trusting children than the sixteenth verse, "Ought not this woman, being a daughter of Abraham, whom Satan hath bound, lo, these eighteen years, be loosed from this bond on the Sabbath day?" This word "ought" expresses much more than willingness. It expresses obligation, right, something which it would be wrong not to do. It places divine healing on a very high and solid plane as not only a possible and actual intervention of God for the help of His suffering children, but as

His normal provision for the believer; something that is included in our redemption rights,
something that is part of the Gospel of His
grace; something that is already recognized
as within His will and not requiring a special
revelation to justify us in claiming it. If God
expects us to do what we ought to do, surely
we may expect as much from Him. There is
something startling in the positiveness and
force with which this is here expressed and
surely no trusting child of God should ever
doubt again His perfect readiness to help and
heal.

THE SACREDNESS OF DIVINE HEALING.

The reason the Lord Jesus healed on the
Sabbath so frequently appears to have been to
lift it out of the plane of a mere material work
and place it on the level of the other spiritual
blessings of the Gospel. The Pharisee, like
our modern materialists, looked upon the healing of sickness as a piece of work very much
like the mending of a broken chair. "There
are six days," he said, "in which men ought
to work; in them come and be healed, not on
the Sabbath day." Therefore the Lord pur-
posely healed on the Sabbath day that He

might lift the healing of the body from a work
of human professionalism to a spiritual experience and a heavenly blessing. It is the experience of most of those who have felt the
Lord's touch upon their bodies that it has a
spiritual value even greater than a physical
benefit. The health and strength we receive
from God does not seek for its exercise in
worldly pleasure and sensual indulgence, but
in holy service for God and our fellow-men.
The health and vigor the Holy Spirit imparts
reach out for the highest ministries and bring
to the heart a spiritual quickening and a realization of the Lord's presence and grace which
we value much more than the relief from pain
or infirmity. Nothing makes Christ so intensely personal as to know Him as the very
life of our conscious being and our material
organism. God has made our body a trinity
and there is an interdependence between spirit,
soul and body which we cannot ignore. The
presence of disease is a hindrance not only to
our spiritual usefulness but to our higher experiences, and while divine healing is not the
greatest blessing of the Gospel, it is a part of
it and has a reflex influence on every other
part of our nature.

12

DIVINE HEALING AND FAITH.

While the Lord is willing to heal yet this passage clearly teaches us that there is a distinct responsibility upon us to claim His healing by definite and aggressive faith. He did not go to her and press upon her His healing touch until she had first reached out to meet Him in response to His call. When Jesus saw her, He called her to Him and said: "Woman, thou art loosed from thine infirmity." He had not yet touched her or even approached her, but He announced to her the great fact of divine power and summoned her to meet it by going to Him. Remember that "she was bound together and could in no wise lift herself up" but the moment that word came to her it constituted her authority to claim deliverance and to put on His strength and step out to meet Him. This she did. Somehow she crossed that synagogue until she came to where He was. Somehow that crippled form took hold of new life and strength until she stood erect or crawled across the intervening space and acted as if His word were already true Then it was that "He laid His hands upon her and she was made straight and glorified God." His actual touch followed her act of faith. She had already taken the healing and all that was needed was for Him to complete it by the actual manifestation. So still we must go out to meet God. We have not to do this in the dark and without His hands being extended first to us. His word to her, "Thou art loosed from thine infirmity," was authority enough for her to act upon. It was just as when He said to the paralytic, "Son, thy sins are forgiven thee." But the paralytic must believe and receive that word before it could be made good to him, and so this woman must believe what the Lord had declared and act as if it were true, and when she did this He followed it with the fulness of He is power and blessing. The reason we are not receiving more help from God is because we are waiting for something first to come to us in our physical senses as a manifestation of God's presence and help. This is inverting the Divine order. We must first believe without sight or sign and then will come the vindication of faith and the touch of God.

THE RIGHTS OF FAITH.

The question naturally arises: Has everybody the right thus to claim deliverance from sickness? Certainly not. This passage only teaches that the believer may claim the Lord's healing. "Ought not this woman, being a daughter of Abraham, to be loosed? " A daughter of Abraham is a daughter of faith. "They that be of faith, the same are the children of Abraham." It is the one who believes in the Lord for healing to whom the promise of healing applies. Surely, this truth is very obviously taught in the great commission in the sixteenth chapter of the Gospel of Mark. The modified translation of that passage as given by Dr. Robert Young brings this out very clearly. "Signs shall follow them that believe these things." In the old version it is "These signs shall follow them that believe." This, however, is not really true for the signs of healing do not follow all believers, but they follow those who believe for the signs. It is the law of the New Testament just as binding as the laws of nature and the great law of the fitness of things "According to thy faith be it unto you." How very solemn is the position in which all this places us. The Lord throws down to us the gauntlet and if we dare to take it up we may have accordingly. There is a fine force in that passage, Luke x. 19, "Behold, I give you authority to tread on serpents and scorpions and over all the power of the enemy." We quite miss the meaning of this when we fail to translate it by the right word "authority." It is not power that He gives us. We do not have the power. He has the power. But He gives us authority to act as if we had the power and then He backs it up with His power. It is like the officer of the law stepping out before a mob and acting in the name of the government. His single word is stronger than a thousand men because he has authority and all the power of the government is behind him.

So faith steps out in the name of heaven and expects God to stand by it, and as we thus stand we shall not be disappointed.

Beloved reader, are you living up to your redemption rights or are you letting them go by default?

CHAPTER XIV.

THE SUFFERINGS OF THE SON OF MAN.

"Who in the days of His flesh, when He had offered up prayers and supplications with strong crying and tears unto Him that was able to save Him from death, and was heard in that He feared" (Heb. v. 7).

THE picture which Luke gives us of the sufferings of Christ is characteristic and touching.

HIS ANTICIPATION OF HIS SUFFERINGS AND LONGING FOR SYMPATHY.

"And He said unto them: With desire I have desired to eat this passover with you before I suffer" (Luke xxii. 15).

The shadow of the cross was falling upon Him and His spirit shrank from the strange horror of a great darkness. He clung closer to His beloved disciples and longed for their fellowship. This sacred feast which He was now instituting was to be through the coming death. With deep tenderness, He took the ages a commemoration of His sufferings and cup and passed it on and down the line of

ages, and one day He is going to take it back
again when the line shall be completed and He
shall drink it anew with all the company of
the ransomed in the kingdom of the Father.

HIS MESSAGE TO SIMON.

"And the Lord said, Simon, Simon, behold,
Satan hath desired to have you, that he may
sift you as wheat: but I have prayed for thee,
that thy faith fail not: and when thou art
converted, strengthen thy brethren" (Luke
xxii. 31, 32).

Here again we see a fine touch of His perfect humanity in His tender sympathy with
His people in their temptations. What a fearful picture He gives of the ravening lion who
goes about seeking whom he may devour and
how vividly Peter himself has reproduced the
figure in his own epistle as he warns his brethren against "that roaring lion who walketh
about seeking whom he may devour." As the
wild beast shakes its victim until it is shaken
to death, so the devil was waiting to shake
Simon and his brethren in his fierce and cruel
hate. The figure of the sieve is most sugges-
tive. The process of sifting throws out everything that is good and leaves behind nothing
but the chaff. Satan's object is to shake out

of us all goodness, all faith and hope and leave us a desolated ruin.

But how unsefish the Master's love. He had already anticipated Peter's danger. He had already prayed for him through his fearful test. "I have prayed for thee that thy faith fail not." But Peter was not to be delivered without his own earnest co-operation. He was not to be carried like a baby or an invalid, but was to stand upon his own feet and triumph by his own faith. That prayer of Christ saved Peter from the fate of Judas. Oh, that we might have the same spirit as the Master and stand with one another in the hard places of life, saying to the tempted and tried, "I have prayed for thee that thy faith fail not!"

THE AGONY IN THE GARDEN.

"And there appeared an angel unto Him from heaven, strengthening Him. And being in an agony He prayed more earnestly: and His sweat was as it were great drops of blood falling down to the ground" (Luke xxii. 43, 44).

What a realistic picture of mental anguish leading to physical suffering and exhaustion and of the dependence of the suffering Saviour upon heavenly relief as the angel came to

strengthen Him.   The mystery of that agony
has been often approached by reverent minds
who have sought to fathom its awful meaning.
Far be it from us to presume to dictate, but
let us ask our readers to consider well the
parallel passage in Heb. v. 7 which describes
this season of mysterious suffering.   The common idea is that our Lord was praying against
the cup of anguish which He was about to
drink as the Saviour and Substitute of sinful
men, and that His human nature, shrinking
from the fearful draught, was seeking if possible some way of escape consistent with His
Father's will, and finally, when that could not
be, His higher will yielded complete submission and His prayer remained unanswered.

In this view, Christ's agony in the garden is
simply a pattern to us of submission to the
will of God when our prayers too remain unanswered.

But when we turn to this passage in Hebrews we find that His prayer was answered,
He "was heard in that He feared."   We are
told also that what He asked for was to be
saved from death.   There can be no doubt
that the passage in Hebrews refers to the
agony in the garden.   There is no other incident in the Saviour's life that could, by any

means, be adjusted to that reference. Now when we turn to the Gospel narrative, we find as Christ entered the garden that an awful shadow fell upon Him, and He cried out, "My soul is exceeding sorrowful even unto death." We find Him also saying a little before, "This is your hour and the power of darkness." Putting all this together, it would really seem as if the adversary had made a fierce attack upon our Lord in the garden with the purpose of destroying Him before the time and so prevent His voluntary offering of His own life a little later on the cross. We know that Christ always had regard about what He called His "time." "My time is not yet come," and He frequently avoided the plots of His enemies as they sought to destroy Him before His time had come.

It would seem therefore as though Satan had made one last terrific onslaught with the purpose of taking His life there and then in the garden of Gethsemane, and that it was against this that Jesus pleaded and struggled and "was heard in that He feared." His life was preserved. An angel appeared strengthening Him and He rose up and went forward with the remaining duties and sufferings of those last hours and at last laid down His own life on the cross according to His previous announcement, "No man taketh it from Me; I have power to lay it down of Myself and I have power to take it again." In this view, the incident is full of encouragement and inspiration. We too are subjected to the attacks of our cruel enemy who would often seek to crush us before our work is done, but in the strength of Him who suffered there we also may overcome and finish our life work so that we shall have "nothing to do but to die."

HIS LOOK UPON PETER.

"And the Lord turned and looked upon Peter. And Peter remembered the word of the Lord, how He had said unto Him, Before the cock crow, thou shalt deny me thrice" (Luke xxii. 61).

All the evangelists make much of our Saviour's expression of countenance. There must have been something very significant in His look on the present occasion. There was everything to give that look a tender and awful meaning. The disciple, whom He had forewarned, was at that very moment rudely and brutally denying Him and even insulting His very name, and just a moment before the signal that the Master had given him had fallen upon his ear with the crowing of the cock in the adjacent yard. That look must have meant not only the severest reproach but the most tender compassion. It must instantly have carried back Peter's though to what the Master had said at the supper table and reminded him of the promise, "I have prayed for thee that thy faith fail not." Hastening from the court and overwhelmed with his conflicting feelings, Peter burst into tears of reproach, penitence and unspeakable sorrow. But that look had saved him from despair and, instead of Judas and his awful fate, Peter comes back again a little later to receive the forgiveness of his Lord and to be more than reinstated in his old place of trust and service. How tenderly that look has been interpreted by John Newton in its application to us in our personal dealing with the Saviour:

> "I saw One hanging on a tree
>   In agony and blood,
> He fixed His dying eyes on me
>   As near the cross I stood.
>
> "Sure, never till my latest breath
>   Can I forget that look;
> It seemed to charge me with His death
>   Though not a word He spoke.

"A second look He gave which said:
    I truly all forgive,
My life is for thy ransom paid,
    I died that thou mayest live."

HIS MESSAGE TO THE DAUGHTERS OF JERUSALEM

"But Jesus turning unto them said, Daughters of Jerusalem, weep not for Me, but weep for yourselves and for your children. For behold, the days are coming, in which they shall say, Blessed are the barren, and the wombs that never bare, and the paps which never gave suck. Then shall they begin to say to the mountains, Fall on us; and to the hills, Cover us. For if they do these things in a green tree, what shall be done in the dry?" (Luke xxiii. 28-31).

What finer picture could we have of unselfish suffering? In the hour of His extremity, the Master was lifted above His own terrible situation by the thought of the greater peril of these loving and sympathizing women who were weeping for His fate. To His loving heart, the sufferings which He was about to endure were simply a measure of the sufferings which they should have to bear for the guilt of rejecting Him, and He added the terrific figure, "If these things be done in a green

tree, what shall be done in the dry?" Briefly
paraphrased, this figure means: "If I, innocent,
and dear to God, the Father's beloved Son,
am going through such an awful tragedy when
I stand in the place of sinful men, how much
worse shall be the sufferings of sinful men
themselves who reject My salvation when they
stand for themselves in the place of the judgment they deserve?" The sufferings of Jesus
Christ are an awful measure of the sinners'
peril and doom and the most fearful expression yet which the Father's judgment has represented is the "wrath of the Lamb."

HIS PRAYER FOR THE FORGIVENESS OF HIS MURDERERS.

"Then said Jesus: Father forgive them for
they know not what they do" (Luke xxiii. 34).

This is peculiar of Luke. How beautifully
it is in keeping with the gracious spirit of His
Gospel as a revelation of the mercy of God.
He had taught His disciples to love their
enemies and pray for them that "despitefully
used them" and now it is His turn to live it
out Himself and to show that even under the
most fearful pressure it is possible to love and
to forgive, but it is only possible if we have
the spirit of that Christ Himself dwelling in

us. Here human nature utterly fails and only the heart of Christ within us can meet the great demand of such a love. Was the prayer of Christ fulfilled? Certainly it was, as was witnessed in the multitudes that were saved on the day of Pentecost and the conversion of Saul himself, the most bitter of all His enemies.

What a beautiful picture it gives us of Christ. He tries to find something extenuating even in the worst of men. "They know not what they do," He cries. His love will discover some excuse or palliation. Truly, there is no love like the love of Jesus. Oh, for a heart like His!

THE COMMITTAL OF HIS SPIRIT TO THE FATHER.

"And when Jesus had cried with a loud voice, He said, Father, into Thy hands I commend My spirit: and having said thus, He gave up the ghost" (Luke xxiii. 46).

The loud voice of which this verse speaks was not used to utter this final prayer, but rather to shout the previous words "it is finished" which John has related as His dying utterance.

That was a shout of victory as He announced to the universe that His work was accomplished and His victory won. But now, doubtless, His voice sinks to a whisper and into His Father's ear alone He breathes this dying prayer, "Father, into Thy hands I commend My Spirit." How beautifully it proves the voluntariness of Christ's sufferings. He gave up His own spirit. The devil tried to take it, but failed, and now victorious He yields it Himself. How clearly it also teaches the immortality of the spirit. There is something in us that cannot die. It is said of Him, "Being put to death in the flesh but quickened in the spirit." A moment after death, His spirit was more active than before and so shall ours be. Oh brother, where?

Finally, what a pattern for the dying saint. His work all done; his warfare accomplished; every promise fulfilled and nothing left but

"On Jesus' breast to lean his head
And breathe his life out sweetly there."

CHAPTER XV.

THE SON OF MAN IN HIS RESUR-
RECTION LIFE.

"But they constrained Him saying, Abide with us: for it is toward evening, and the day is far spent. And He went in to tarry with them" (Luke xxiv. 29).

THE story of the walk to Emmaus which Luke has told us with such graphic simplicity, has left a picture of the risen Christ upon the heart of the church of Christ unequalled by any other record of the resurrection. There is something about it that reminds one of one of those Indian summer days that come to us as a transition between the summer and winter, a sort of second summer and yet with a mystic glory about it that seems to belong to some other clime.

The Christ of the Forty Days, as represented in this picture, while the same in Person as the old Christ of Judea and Galilee has risen to a new plane, more spiritual, more mysterious and more supernatural. He was lifting their thoughts to that heavenly fellowship which they were henceforth to have with Him and yet losing none of the old humanness and tenderness they had known so well. Let us gather out of this story of Emmaus some of the points of light which it sheds upon the Christ of to-day.

WE SEE THE EVER PRESENT CHRIST.

He who came to them that day still comes to us as we walk the path of life. He is an everlasting Presence, an ever present Friend and His gentle voice whispers down the ages, "Lo, I am with you all the days even unto the end of the age." Just as simply, just as naturally as He drew nigh to them, so

> "Still through all life's way He walketh
> Ever near our side."

HE IS THE RISEN CHRIST.

There is a new touch to His humanity. It has passed through the grave and come forth transformed, transfigured and glorified. Speaking of Him, the Apostle Paul says: "Though I have known Christ after the flesh, yet now henceforth know I Him no more."

As Mary clasped Him by the feet and tried to hold Him in the old relationship, He tenderly reminded her "Touch me not; I ascend unto My Father and your Father." She was to have a higher touch and recognize Him as in a new place of spiritual manifestation and communion.

WE SEE THE CHRIST WHO OFTEN WALKS WITH US UNRECOGNIZED.

They did not know Him at first. How often He is with us unknown, and it is not until His Presence has passed and we recall how our hearts burned within us that we wake with the joyful cry, "It was the Lord." Many a providence, many an answer to prayer, many a human touch brings Him near, and when we seem most alone He is often closest to our side.

WE SEE IN THIS INCIDENT A CHRIST WHO KNOWS OUR EVERY CIRCUMSTANCE AND CONDITION AND ADJUSTS HIMSELF TO OUR LIFE.

He dropped into their conversation. He noticed that they were sad. He took up the thread of life and wove it into a message of wondrous blessing. So He comes to us just where we are. We do not need to climb to strained spiritual planes to bring the Lord Christ down. There is nothing with which He cannot blend and into which He cannot bring His loving companionship.

"There's no time too busy for His leisure,
  There's no task too hard for His to bear,
There's no soul too lowly for His notice,
  There's no need too trifling for His care.

There's no place too lonely for His presence,
  There's no pain His bosom cannot feel,
There's no sorrow that He cannot comfort,
  There's no sickness that He cannot heal."

HE SPEAKS TO US THROUGH HIS WORD.

"Beginning at Moses and all the prophets, He expounded unto them in all the Scriptures the things concerning Himself." And so He still comes to us through His Word. If we knew it better and studied it more, we should find the blessed Christ ever ready to meet us through its glowing pages and to speak to us through its exceeding great and precious promises. "The testimony of Jesus is the spirit of prophecy." Have we learned to recognize His face on every page and His voice in every promise?

HE MAKES OUR HEART TO BURN WITHIN US AS
HE OPENS TO US THE SCRIPTURES.

His Word is not mere intellectual light, but spiritual life and celestial fire. It is the eyes of our heart that need to be enlightened more than the faculties of our understanding. It is little use to read the Bible simply as a duty or a study. We want to read it with burning hearts and glowing love as the love letter of His affection and the mirror of His face.

BUT THE LORD WANTS A CLOSER INTIMACY THAN EVEN THE REVELATION OF HIS WORD.

He longs to reveal Himself to the loving heart by a personal visitation and manifestation. And so, as they came to their destination at the village of Emmaus, He allowed them to constrain Him to enter in. There is something fondly playful and intensely human in the statement that He "made as though He would have gone further." But this was only because He wanted to be pressed. He would not stay as an unwelcome guest. He wanted their insistent love and was willing to be constrained. He will not break into our hearts or force open any door. "Behold, I stand at the door and knock," He cries, "if any man will hear My voice and open the door, I will come into him and sup with him and he with Me." Therefore He sometimes holds back the answer to our prayer and the revelation of His face that our desire may be deepened and our appeal may be pressed more lovingly upon

His heart. But when He saw that He was welcome, how glad He was to respond.

How touching their appeal! "Abide with us for it is toward evening and the day is far spent." How that loving appeal has echoed through the ages as the cry of lonely hearts longing for the Saviour's Presence. How often since has that prayer ascended from the lonely, the sorrowing, the oppressed and the sinking soul! Never can it go up in vain to His loving heart. Just as in nature, the warm currents of the atmosphere rush to fill the vacuum, so the hungry and the empty heart will always find the Saviour near. "He satisfieth the longing heart and filleth the hungry with good things." There is in every Christian experience a reality corresponding to the scene at Emmaus. The Lord Jesus does come and make Himself real to the loving and longing soul. "If a man love Me he will keep My words and I will love him and manifest Myself unto him."

When He came into the house at Emmaus, He was no longer the shy and disguised Stranger, but immediately took His place and made Himself known. Sitting at the head of the table, He took the bread and blessed and brake and as together they partook we read,

"Their eyes were opened and they knew Him."
The old smile of recognition could not be mistaken. It was their own blessed Lord, their
precious Christ, and their hearts were filled
with joy, with a joy so deep that He was constrained to withdraw the vision and vanish
from their sight.

THE VANISHING VISION.

He vanished out of their sight. This was
deeply significant. Had He lingered longer,
the whole meaning of His new relation to them
would have been mistaken. Henceforth it was
to be by faith and not by sight. There was a
moment of vision and the memory of sight, but
now they must rise up and walk by simple
faith and go forth by the dead reckoning of a
life of trust. It is unwholesome to be always
looking for spiritual feeling and emotional joy.
The normal atmosphere and attitude of the
Christian is trust and the fellowship of prayer.
"We walk by faith and not by sight." How
slow they were to learn this lesson! How, on
another occasion, the doubting Thomas even
demanded that he should have some outward
sign of the Master's Presence and how the
Lord reproved him, even as He granted it:
"Thomas, because thou hast seen thou hast be-

lieved; blessed are they who have not seen and yet have believed." Let us not miss the blessing but learn to go forth leaning upon His Word, counting upon His unseen Presence and by steadfast faith testifying with the Psalmist, "I have set the Lord alway before me; because He is at my right hand I shall not be moved." Someone has written a helpful leaflet on the practice of the Presence of God, and this is a spiritual exercise which we may most profitably pursue. A distinguished preacher tells how every morning as he sits down in his library, he places a chair for the Master to sit by his side, and all through the hours of study they talk together, pray together, plan together the work of the day, and when he goes forth to life's more public duties, he is conscious, not of any ecstatic vision or any supernatural revelation, but an atmosphere illumined and fragrant with the breath of heaven and a heart all aglow from the Presence and fellowship of the Lord.

Shall we thus go forth to walk with Him until the gates of vision open at last and we shall see His face and be with Him in the glory?

'Tis so sweet to walk with Jesus
  Step by step and day by day,
Stepping in His very footprints,
  Walking with Him all the way.

Soon with all who walk with Jesus
  We shall walk with Him in white,
While He turns our grief to gladness
  And our darkness into light.

Jesus, keep me closer, closer,
  Step by step and day by day,
Stepping in Thy very footprints,
  Walking with Thee all the way.

Chapter XVI.

THE PARTING SCENES.

"And He led them out as far as to Bethany, and He lifted up His hands, and blessed them.

"And it came to pass, while He blessed them, He was parted from them and carried up into heaven." (Luke xxiv. 50, 51.)

AFTER the meeting with the Lord at Emmaus, the two disciples returned immediately to Jerusalem to tell to their brethren the joyful news that the Lord had appeared to them. But as they entered the closed upper chamber, they were anticipated by the greeting, "The Lord is risen indeed and hath appeared unto Simon." We have no particulars of this meeting with Simon except the hint which the Lord Himself gave in His first meeting with the woman, "Tell Peter," and also the reference by the Apostle Paul in I. Cor. xv. 5, "He was seen of Cephas." Somewhere and some time that morning He had met the broken-hearted disciple and passed some confidential word that never has been told to other ears. Then the two disciples told their story of the walk to Emmaus and the meeting there, but even while they spake, the Lord Himself

appeared, entering through the closed doors
and suddenly standing in their presence. From
the mysterious shadow form, they shrank back
with dread and took it for an apparition. But
immediately His re-assuring voice declared,
"Why are ye troubled and why do thoughts
arise in your heart; behold My hands and My
feet that it is I Myself, handle Me and see, for
a spirit hath not flesh and bones as ye see Me
have." And then, still further to re-assure
them, for we are told, "They yet believed not
for joy and wondered," He called for food
and ate before them a piece of broiled fish and
a honey-comb which probably was left from
their evening meal. No longer could they
doubt that it was indeed their Lord Himself
strangely changed in many things and yet the
very same Jesus.

THE MANIFESTATION.

Nowhere in the records of the resurrection
have we a picture at all approaching in realistic vividness this picture of the risen Christ.
Speculation must, of course, curb all irreverent
or presumptuous boldness in attempting to de-
fine and describe the resurrection life of our
blessed Lord, and yet there are touches of intense humanness here which the Holy Spirit

surely intended that we should realize and
draw comfort and inspiration from. While on
the one hand, there is much that is mysterious and supernatural and His body was posses-
sed of powers that belong to a higher sphere
of human life, passing at will through closed
doors, transporting Himself in a moment to
distant places and rising by the impulse of His
own will without effort, in spite of the law of
gravitation, until His glorified body floated
away into space; while all this is true, yet on
the other hand the print of the nails and the
mark of the spear were still apparent. His
corporeal frame was tangible to the touch of
their hands and He insisted that they should
examine and handle and see. There were
bones and flesh in His material form. It was
an actual substance as real as their own bodies.
There would seem to have been an absence of
blood, for He speaks only of flesh and bones.
Was it that the blood was the corruptible mortal
life and that He left it behind as the ransom
for our lives, and that the resurrection body
has some higher vital fluid than the blood
which sustains our life? While He did not
need the nourishment of food, yet He could
eat the broiled fish. He could taste the sweetness of the honey-comb. He could share any

of the physical attributes of our humanity. How gloriously real all this makes the Christ to us. This Man with a body like our own has passed out of sight, but not out of existence. He is still the same Jesus and will forever be the most glorious and perfect Representative of our humanity. This Body is the Head of our body and from it we can draw the physical strength and life we need. It was of this He was speaking in the sixth chapter of John when he said, "As the living Father hath sent Me and I live by the Father, so he that eateth Me even he shall live by Me." And when they wondered how any one could eat His flesh and drink His blood, He explained that all this was to be made plain after His resurrection; that it was in His risen body that this was to be fulfilled. "What and if ye shall see the Son of man ascend up where He was before; it is the spirit that quickeneth, the flesh profiteth nothing. The words that I speak unto you, they are spirit and they are life" (John vi. 62-63).

Beloved reader, have you learned to draw your life from this living One and find in Him the source of strength for every physical as well as every spiritual need?

This glorified Christ is also the pattern and

type of our glorified humanity. As He is, so shall we some day be. "As the earthy is, so are they also that are earthy, and as are the heavenly, so are they also that are heavenly, and as we have borne the image of the earth so we shall also bear the image of the heavenly." Into the fullness of this glorified life, humanity cannot enter until after the resurrection, and yet even now "the spirits of just men made perfect" doubtless enter into a very real and conscious blessedness waiting for the fullness of their glory when He shall be revealed as our coming Lord and King. "It doth not yet appear what we shall be, but we know that when He shall appear, we shall be like Him for we shall see Him as He is."

THE ILLUMINATION.

This brings us back to more ordinary planes. His manifested Presence may not be always visible, but there is one place where we can always find Him and that is in His holy Word. And so He immediately began to give them the key to the Scriptures and make it possible for them henceforth always to find Him there. "These are the words which I spake unto you while I was yet present with you," He says, "that all things must be fulfilled which were written in the law of Moses and in the Prophets and in the Psalms concerning Me." It is remarkable that He uses the same general division of the old Scriptures which was used among the rabbis. The Law was the first division containing the writings of Moses. The Prophets constituted the next division containing the historical portions and the prophetic Scriptures. And the Psalms finished the sub-division including not only the Psalms of David, but the other poetical books of the Bible, Job, Proverbs, Song of Solomon, etc. And so He takes up the three divisions and gives them a lesson in Bible study, the details of which are not recorded, but the substance of which no doubt forever remained in their minds and hearts as the foundation principles of the entire New Testament teaching.

It is not difficult for us, in view of the deeper teachings of the apostles, to imagine the substance of that wondrous message which they heard for the first time that day from the Risen Christ. How their hearts must have burned as He explained to them the sacrifice of Abel, the offering of Isaac on Mt. Moriah, the blood of the Pascal Lamb, the wondrous types of the Jewish Tabernacle, the great High Priest and his robes and functions, the Day

of Atonement, the Scapegoat and all the
bloody sacrifices and varied offerings of the
Mosaic economy. And then would follow the
prophetic psalms, the 53rd chapter of Isaiah
and the varied pictures of the coming Messiah
in Jeremiah, Zechariah, Malachi and the
other prophets until at last they understood
that "thus it was written and thus it behooved Christ to suffer and to rise from the
dead the third day."

But a lamp was as necessary as a key for
the full understanding of the sacred volume,
and so we read, "Then opened He their understanding that they might understand the Scriptures." Oh! What a light shines upon the
sacred page when the Holy Spirit reveals to
the hungry heart that wondrous Face that
shines on every page of the prophetic Word
and the truth becomes clear that "The testimony of Jesus is the spirit of prophecy."

The story is told of some children who were
trying to make the pieces of a mechanical map
fit together. Vainly and patiently they adjusted the blocks, but they could not get the
lines rightly to meet or the counties and coun-
tries to fit into their places. At length one of
them turned over some of the blocks and
noticed a picture on the other side, "Why," he

said, "here is a picture of George Washington on the back of the blocks. Let's try and fit that together." This was an easier task, and it was not long until George Washington stood out from the floor in the little Mosaic picture of one hundred blocks, a perfect figure. Then it occurred to them to turn over the blocks, leaving them exactly where they were, and as they did so, lo! the map was complete. The face of the man was the key to the adjustment of the map. In a far higher sense, it is true that the Lord Jesus Christ is the key to the whole Bible. Study it scientifically, philosophically, theologically, critically and you will never be satisfied, but put the pieces together until there stands out the face and form of Jesus Christ, and lo, the problem is solved, the message is plain, the Book is simple as A. B. C. and sweet as the very heart of love.

Dear reader, have you learned this solution of the mysteries of the Bible? Has it become to you the

"Love letter of your Bridegroom's heart,
    And mirror of your Saviour's face."

THE COMMISSION.

Now comes the Master's commission for their ministry and service, "And that repent-

ance and remission of sins should be preached
in His name among all nations beginning at
Jerusalem, and ye are witnesses of these
things." This is the proclamation of a universal amnesty for the whole human family, and
especially for the Jewish nation which had
crucified Him. He now authorizes them to go
forth and proclaim through His name forgiveness to every abandoned soul throughout the
whole wide world and to begin with His very
murderers. The remarkable feature about this
is that the message to Israel is here committed to the Gentiles. Luke is the Gospel, not
for the Jew, but for the Gentile, and the fact
that this commission should be found here
rather than in Matthew is most significant.

Have we Gentile Christians been true to our
trust for Israel and have we given the message "to the Jew first and also to the Greek?"
Through every generation this is our first responsibility: to offer this risen Christ to the
men whose fathers crucified Him and to leave
upon each.individual the responsibility of accepting or rejecting Him, one by one. Have
we been faithful to this trust as opportunity
has come to us and the brethren of our Lord,
according to the flesh, have crossed our earthly
path? They will not all accept it. A strange

veil is upon their hearts. We will often wonder at the indifference and hardness of heart that seems to coolly ignore the call of their Saviour, but all the same He wants us to give them the message, to afford them an opportunity and to leave upon them the responsibility of accepting or rejecting Him. Some time they will meet Him again when He comes in glory and when there will be no doubt left upon their minds that He is their rejected Messiah and then their eternal future will hang upon the question, "How did you treat the message of salvation which My servants brought you in the days of time?"

THE PROMISE OF THE SPIRIT.

For this great trust that He is committing to them, He now promises to them a special divine equipment and enduement. "Behold, I send the promise to My Father upon you, but tarry ye in the City of Jerusalem until ye be endued with power from on high." He calls it "the promise." It is indeed the promise inclusive of every other for everything that the Christian's heart can need is summed up in the Holy Ghost. Do we want cleansing and purity? He is the Spirit of holiness. Do we want joy and peace? All true joy is in the Holy

Ghost. Would we have our hearts fired by
love? "The love of God is shed abroad in our
hearts by the Holy Ghost which He hath given
to us." Is it power for service? "Ye shall receive power after that the Holy Ghost is come
upon you." Would we know how to pray until
our prayers bring an answer from above?
"The Spirit maketh intercession within us with
groanings which cannot be uttered." "The
Spirit helpeth our infirmities." There is nothing which is not covered by the promise of the
Holy Ghost.

Dear reader, have you claimed, have you received the promise of the Father? This is
spoken of also as an enduement. The word
"endue" means clothe. It is not a personal
characteristic or a result of culture and education. It is a direct, divine enabling. When
the Holy Spirit comes to us, the power He
gives is not our power, but His. We wear it
as a robe, recognizing Him as the source and
maintaining the attitude of personal dependence by simple faith. They were bidden to
tarry until they should be endued with power
from on high. This does not imply in our case
that God is not immediately ready to give us
the blessing of the Spirit, but we are not always ready. The tarrying prepares our hearts

to receive Him, shows to us our deeper need, enables us to put aside the things that hinder and makes room for the deeper and fuller blessing. Have we met these practical conditions? Have we claimed the promise of the Spirit? Have we been endued with power from on high? Are we in the attitude of tarrying and habitually waiting on the Lord for the fresh anointing which we need for every new service and emergency?

THE PARTING.

At length the hour for parting comes. There is no announcement that He is to leave them, but perhaps there is an instinct such as that which came to Elisha before his master was taken up into heaven. But apparently it is as at other times as He appears to them and leads them out as far as to Bethany. We are not told that it was exactly at Bethany, but it was in that vicinity, and as far from Jerusalem. He was still talking to them and His hands were raised in benediction as had often been the case before at His partings, but now, as He blesses them, He gradually rises before their very eyes, calmly majestic, with His face shining with love, His eyes perhaps moist with tears, His hands still stretched out in benediction, higher and higher and higher while their strained eyes follow Him with intense, absorbing attention until a floating cloud intervened and He had disappeared behind it and they woke from the spell to realize that at last He had gone away into heaven. What words could express the sweet and solemn fragrance of that last parting attitude and those extended hands above their heads in loving benediction. As He blessed them He was parted from them. Their last sight of Him was an attitude of blessing. He had come with blessing. His Sermon on the Mount had opened with nothing but beatitudes. His messages were always love and now His last act was blessing. Some day, when He comes again, He will take up the echo once more and His words will be, "Come, ye blessed of My Father, inherit the kingdom prepared for thee from the foundation of the world."

Oh! dear reader, are you included in that blessing? It is for all that will accept Him and the only curse which yonder heavens hold for mortals is a fearful anathema on those that do not love Him. God save you from ever coming under the lightning breath of this fearful curse, "If any man love not the Lord Jesus, let Him be anathema maranatha," that is, accursed when the Lord shall come.